Durations

A Memoir and Personal Essays

Other Works by Carolyn Osborn

A Horse of Another Color

The Fields of Memory

The Grands

Warriors & Maidens

Uncertain Ground

Contrary People

Where We Are Now

Durations

A Memoir and Personal Essays

Carolyn Osborn

To Wayne From Carolyn Osborne March 26, 2022

WingsPress

San Antonio, Texas
2017

Durations: a memoir and personal essays © 2017 by Carolyn Osborn

Cover design by Barbara Whitehead, based on a black and white picture by Catherine Osborn. Unless noted otherwise, all photographs © 2017 by Carolyn Osborn.

ISBN: 978-1-60940-544-1 (paperback original)

E-books:
epub: 978-1-60940-545-8
Mobipocket/Kindle: 978-1-60940-546-5
Library PDF: 978-1-60940-547-2

Wings Press
627 E. Guenther
San Antonio, Texas 78210
Phone/fax: (210) 271-7805
On-line catalogue and ordering:
www.wingspress.com

Wings Press books are distributed to the trade by
Independent Publishers Group
www.ipgbook.com

Library of Congress Cataloging-in-Publication Data:

Names: Osborn, Carolyn, 1934- author.
Title: Durations : a memoir and personal essays / Carolyn Osborn.
Description: San Antonio, Texas : Wings Press, 2017.
Identifiers: LCCN 2017005581| ISBN 9781609405441 (softcover : acid-free
paper) | ISBN 9781609405465 (kindle/mobipocket ebook) | ISBN 9781609405472
(library pdf)
Classification: LCC PS3565.S348 A6 2017 | DDC 814/.54--dc23
LC record available at https://lccn.loc.gov/2017005581

"Durations" was partially published in *Antioch Review* and *Southern Cultures*. Essays previously published include "Sheep May Safely Graze" in *American Literary Review*, "My Father's Guns," in *Hotel Amerika*, "Ranching on Dry Ground," in *Missouri Review*, "Under Guard" and "Mingling With the Scots" in *Southwest Review*, and "The Galapagos: A Booby Tour" in *Antioch Review*.

Contents

Durations: A Memoir

Essays

Durations

Durations

I.

Shelters

When World War II began in 1941 my brother was five and I was seven. Though we had no premonitions of ever being without parents, before the war was over we lived without them. Fortunately, various branches of our large southern family took us in, so we weren't orphans or foster children. Young as we were, however, we knew a little about orphans, and I believe on some unconscious level we probably feared we might be abandoned as they were.

We could see an orphanage—or Orphans' Home as it was sometimes softened to—in its bleak red brick splendor, a little way off the road we took from our house in Nashville to Grandmother Truett's house in Franklin, Tennessee. Its imposing walls loomed above surrounding fields and trees; a faint grayish haze rising from a nearby river usually gave a murky outline to its outer flanks. We disliked it and we especially disliked having to give our toys away to the orphans. Mother explained since we were moving to Franklin we couldn't carry everything. Our father's army orders had already sent him north to Camp Campbell on the Tennessee-Kentucky border. To obey Mother's charitable impulse, one we certainly didn't share, we slowly filled a cardboard box with toys. Which ones, I have forgotten. Billy kept his teddy bear, I know. He would hug it through moves throughout the war since we went in every direction—west to California, back east to Tennessee, north to Pennsylvania, back south to Tennessee, and finally the ragged bear was packed to go with us west to Texas. The orphans didn't receive my dollhouse either. While all the moving was going on, Mother stored it in the capacious attic of our grandmother's large, white frame Victorian duplex with porches on two sides, both lavishly dripping with gingerbread.

I'd already finished the first grade in Nashville and begun the second. Mother, in this time of great uncertainty, decided to take us and return to her childhood home. Among the families we knew, young women whose husbands had left for service often made such a decision. It might have been done for the sake of economy, but more than that, going home held the comfort of family support. Mother gained her mother's help with us children as well as her company, which could be difficult. Widowed young, my grandmother Truett was an independent, sometimes dominating figure, while my mother had been married and living in a house she and my father had chosen in Nashville for eight years. They were bound to clash. According to other family members, they did, but Billy and I never heard those quarrels. The rule in that house, "Not in front of the help or the children," prevailed. Yet more compelling than any discomfort, I've come to believe, was Mother's need to flee to a familiar refuge.

When we lived Nashville the short distance to the neighborhood grammar school allowed Mother to drive or walk with me to school everyday. As a second grader, she judged I was old enough to walk, now and then, with the boy across the street in good weather. Once home, Mother allowed us to play only in the backyard within her sight. Perhaps she feared the woods just beyond beckoned. Though wandering didn't attract me, Billy was a born explorer. Since we lived almost on top of a steep hill, she may have felt the front yard, also surrounded by woods on one side, was too dangerous for play without her supervision. Those she loved, she kept near.

Second grade in Franklin didn't last long because the army transferred our father from Camp Campbell to Camp Roberts, near Paso Robles, California. Grandmother Truett got in the car with us and, in the magical way things seem to happen to children, off Mother drove us across more than half the country, stopping to visit a great aunt and uncle in Amarillo. I was fascinated with them, as I'd never seen either one before. To add to their novelty, Great Aunt Leila, said to be half-Indian, with her olive skin, her long dark hair, and her turquoise jewelry, looked the part. To my Grandmother's chagrin—she was an adamant member of the Church of Christ—Great Uncle Gentry owned a liquor store. The fact that her brother dared to oppose Grandmother's beliefs made Uncle Gentry a great wonder although he was a quiet man and, while we were there—as well as every other time I saw him—totally sober. After Amarillo we stopped again to buy Navajo rugs and blankets in New Mexico. Reaching the desert, we had to slow down behind huge army tanks—enormous machines with menacing snouts "on maneuvers," Mother explained. We edged past them as they slowly clanked down the road, while others at a distance wandered in a sandstorm of their own making. Once in California, Grandmother left us to visit her other daughter, Thelma, and her husband, Nelson Griswold, who were living then in San Bernadino. Eventually she returned to Tennessee. War or no, my grandmother was a great traveler; she liked to announce she'd been to thirty-eight states, most of them by train. She left home sneezing from ragweed for Saratoga Springs or some other spa every fall.

We stayed as near to my father's post as possible. Tight housing forced us to share, with another army family, a small ranch house in the country outside Paso Robles, where I was enrolled for my third try at second grade. Somehow I felt threatened by the big, yellow school bus, supposedly my ride from the ranch to town. Mother gave into my complaints and drove me to school. Feeling a vague pity for the children who had to travel inside the monster bus, I waved to them when we passed.

Since the housing situation didn't suit Mother, we moved down the coast to Atascadero where I entered my fourth and final second grade. For a while we lived in a hotel, which had certain advantages, such as not having to make up your bed, but the best was that you could sit down at a counter for breakfast and order whatever struck your fancy. Discovered by my mother with a half a grapefruit with a cherry on top and a milkshake in front of me, I learned I needed to curb my desire for novelty. Billy at last started kindergarten; just as soon as he was taken there for a morning he ran away, the first sign of his continual dislike of school of any kind. Quickly found and returned, he couldn't be made to stay.

In the summer of 1942, after we tried living in a series of small white-frame houses, it seemed we might settle in one not far from the ocean. Whenever my father could get leave, he joined us, usually on weekends, and even then he sometimes wanted to take us somewhere else, to put a distance between himself and his army duties, perhaps to put a greater distance between all of us and the war. With him we went to Santa Barbara where we rented a house near the beach. Listening to the ocean's giant roar, fearing its cold water, Billy and I only dabbled at the edge. Mother watched us while our father stood in the surf and let it pour over him. Another time in San Francisco, leaving our hotel, I somehow let go of Mother's hand and unknowingly took the hand of a woman who'd been walking with her husband immediately in front of us. Disoriented and frightened when I looked up at the strange woman, I turned my head to find my family laughing behind me. I was at first bewildered, then mad at everyone for letting me float away.

"Why did you let me go?" I asked Mother.

"We could see you ahead of us." She laughed again and this time I laughed with her.

Finally, because the war was no nearer being over than it was when we drove to California, my father decided we should go back to Tennessee "for the duration," a phrase much in use which I translated to "nobody knows how long."

Our house in Nashville had been sold, so we stayed with our grandmother once more, but this time the living arrangements were different. Instead of using the upstairs bedrooms since her only brother, Uncle Felix, divorced and living at home, had moved into one of them, Mother got our furniture out of storage and arranged it in the other half of the big old duplex. Here was the familiar bedroom suite given to my father by his grandfather, a mahogany-veneered cluster large enough to fill two rooms, plus our own living and dining room furniture. Between Grandmother's side and ours stood a pair of heavy sliding doors. We saw Grandmother at intervals—it was easy to run out our back door to hers—and we used her porch swing whenever we pleased, but those heavy doors dividing the house were never opened. Living next to, yet apart from her must have been easier for Mother. How Billy fared in Franklin's first grade, I don't know, nor do I have much of a memory of my third grade year there. I know I hated the playground and what seemed to be an eternal game of

Red Rover because my skinny arms ached from holding on so hard while the other team threw someone against mine. Out of the whole school year, I've kept in mind only one other incident. In the spring I was assigned to memorize a poem about a child's dislike of antiques, one I had to recite to an enormous audience of children and parents collected in the school's auditorium. I wasn't afraid of performing, but even as I was saying the poem, I became aware of playacting; I had nothing against antiques. Although my grandmother's horsehair-filled, leather-covered sofa and chairs weren't exactly comfortable, I didn't have to sit on them often.

By July of 1943, after almost a year's stay in Franklin —Mother took us out of school early in May—we were living in Kittanning, Pennsylvania, with a great aunt, Grandmother Truett's sister, Allie, and her husband, Gerald Foster. We'd arrived there on a train so crowded with troops wearing olive-drab uniforms that they stood in the aisles. The pressure of bodies combined with stuffy heat made us miserable. The soldiers said they were on their way "overseas." My brother and I had learned to fear the word; we both grew quiet and quit complaining. Those were terrible days to be traveling anywhere; however our mother insisted we must go. To Billy and me, it was simply a matter of being with Mother wherever she went although it was our second trip halfway across the country in two years. Aunt Allie—I learned later—Mother felt would help her. I've never known how. Perhaps she thought Allie, because of her much avowed Christian faith, had somehow acquired superior insights, and during this hard time in her life, could relieve her. In that period Mother felt acute anxiety about my father, still in California at Camp Roberts, still hoping to join the next battalion going overseas. (He never did. Instead, despite his requests for overseas duty, the army kept him in the U.S. in charge of training five, sometimes six battalions, for combat.) Mother, at thirty-six, also suffered from the onset of a mental illness no one recognized until much later.

Of the time in Kittanning, I have curiously little memory. Our relatives lived in a large, yellow-brick house with a curving front porch on a corner. A wide green river, the Allegheny, ran nearby. Aunt Allie was a fat, dumpling-like woman while Uncle Gerald, noticeably older than she, was a spare white-haired man who wore glasses. He was kindly, I sensed, though he seemed to be living at a little distance from the rest of us.

I'm not certain where Billy and I slept; I know we didn't have rooms of our own. Perhaps, as we were never far from her, we were given smaller beds or cots in Mother's room. On one of those cold early mornings in Pennsylvania, Mother let me crawl in bed with her and told me Grandfather Culbert, my father's father, had died. It was July 12, the day after my ninth birthday. I had never known anyone who'd died; however, I connected this loss with old age, not the kind of death threatening my father.

I said, "You waited till after my birthday to tell me, didn't you?"

"Yes," she admitted. "I did," and hugged me.

A few weeks later Aunt Allie told me, as I passed through the kitchen, "Go talk to your mother. She's sad."

This was the only hint I ever received about something being wrong. I went out to the back concrete steps and sat down beside my mother. I wish I could remember what she said then as those were the last words we spoke to each other for years to come. Instead I remember the hardness of those steps and the soft gray of an approaching twilight, one of memory's usual tricks; to forget what someone said but to keep the surroundings in mind.

Soon after that Billy and I went to a birthday party for a child we must have made friends with who lived nearby. When we returned home, Mother was gone.

"She fainted. An ambulance came and got her. She's in the hospital," said Aunt Allie.

Our father, given compassionate leave, arrived and went to see her. Grandmother Truett came to visit and shortly after took Mother, I discovered much later, to a series of spas. Hydrotherapy, partially involving soaking the patient in cold or warm water, was one of the preferred treatments for anyone who had what was, in those days, called a "nervous breakdown." I've heard the same description used these days as well. During this period, one of many long silences, neither my brother nor I knew when they took Mother out of the hospital and left; nor were we told where she'd gone. Billy—the adults decided—needed male influence, so he stayed in Pennsylvania with Uncle Gerald and Aunt Allie. On a train once again, I left Kittanning with my father to live with his two sisters and his mother in Nashville. I must have been shocked by the loss of Mother as well as the suddenness of the decision to leave since that whole trip is an utter blank while I can easily recall parts of other long trips taken as a child.

The only scene remaining from that trip comes from the end of it when my tall father dropped our suitcases on the porch and rang the bell while I stood reading the brass numbers, 1108, outside the front door of my grandmother Culbert's gray brick house on 18th Avenue South. Soon after I would be given the small job of polishing those numbers. It was hot, mid-July, 1943. World War II was a little over a year and a half old.

We were hardly inside before I was sent out to the backyard.

"Carolyn, why don't you go see the new birdbath," Aunt Elnora said.

I recognized this as one of those questions I wasn't supposed to answer. Even if I couldn't imagine what might be interesting about a birdbath, I did as she suggested. Aunt Elnora, my father's elder sister as well as a schoolteacher, was as accustomed to obedience as my soldier father.

Annie, Grandmother's cook, busy with supper, said the barest hello when I traipsed through the kitchen. I hadn't expected her to say anything much. From prewar visits to my grandparents' house, I knew Annie tended toward grouchiness. She was a fine cook, but neither she nor the vast and largely empty kitchen she ruled were welcoming. The single straight chair, marked by a faded flattened cushion, was hers. A stove stood against one wall, a small refrigerator on another, an enameled table by Annie's chair on the third, and on the fourth, hung a large white enameled sink with permanent rust stains streaking down from the faucets in the tall backsplash. When the house was built in 1910, no one gave much consideration to kitchen design or to the cook. Annie's temper probably wasn't helped by the exhausting amount of walking she had to do in that room.

Through the latticed back porch and down the steps I went to stare at the cream-colored cement birdbath already filled with water. I sat down on a porch step and waited. No birds appeared. Near the birdbath and between two trees was a bare space, and past that stood the large wooden garage sheltering Aunt Elnora's 1934 Pontiac coupe, which I admired for its cleverly concealed rumble seat. Aunt Dorothy had to park her less exotic sedan outside. To my right, slanting toward the house's back wall, were the cellar doors opened only for coal deliveries. The sun looked as if it might be starting down. It seemed the war would never be over. It seemed I would have to wait till dark until the grown-ups were through talking and I could go inside again. I knew what they were talking about—my hospitalized mother—but exactly where she lived and what she was being treated for was a secret. No matter how many times Billy and I asked while we were both in Pennsylvania, we weren't allowed to see her after she disappeared. Her doctors, we were told, said our visits would not help her, nor would they be good for us.

Though puzzled still, we were reassured that she would get better, and we would see her later.

After delivering me to Nashville, my father returned to train troops at Camp Roberts on the west coast. Eventually Billy might be brought to Nashville so we could be together. I hoped he would come, that Mother would soon recover, that the war would be over, that my father would not be sent overseas, and he would return home unharmed. Everyone lived on hope then.

II.

Living With Aunts

Torn down a few years ago to make room for an ugly black asphalt parking lot, 1108, the house my great-grandfather built for his daughter—he oversaw every brick that went into it—no longer exists except in memory. Sometimes I wonder if anyone picked out the two green Rookwood acanthus leaves that were embedded in tile on either side of the fireplace, or if anyone saved the chestnut paneling in my bedroom, or what happened to the wooden cannon ball on the stairway's newel post. Memory clings to certain objects as well as to the floor plans of houses I've lived in; these are so sharply imprinted my dreams incorporate them.

A living area stretched across the first story, the kitchen plus two spaces behind it (one cave-like walk-in closet for canned goods and cooking utensils, one butler's pantry for a non-existent butler with a built-in china closet), back and front porches, a half bath downstairs and a full one upstairs to accommodate the four bedrooms. Above all was a huge floored attic filled with trunks and furniture and lit by a large, multi-paned front window.

In one of the back upstairs bedrooms, Miss Jones, a registered nurse in charge of grandmother, spent her nights. Grandmother, so paralyzed by Parkinson's disease she couldn't speak, lived downstairs in what had been the formal dining room, a door away from the butler's pantry. She slept there, then later was shifted into to a wheelchair, pushed part of each day to the converted living room-dining area or to the front porch in good weather. Aunt Elnora, the elder unmarried daughter who taught eighth grade home economics in East Nashville, had one of the front upstairs bedrooms. My front room, the only one with a fireplace, was between her room and Aunt Dorothy's, the childless younger daughter who worked as a reporter on *The Nashville Tennessean*. Her job she said, "helped me keep my sanity" while her husband, Fred Lucas, remained stationed in India, so far away he was never eligible for home leave. Hattie, the black night nurse, stayed in a screened alcove outside Grandmother's room on the first floor. The only other woman in the household, Annie, went home at night.

On some weekends and often during the summers, whenever invited, I visited cousins on Mother's side of the family in the country or rode a Greyhound bus to see Grandmother Truett, who still lived in Franklin and shared her Victorian duplex there with Aunt Thelma and her husband, Uncle Nelson Griswold, after his insurance company transferred him back home to Tennessee from California. During the rest of the year I walked three blocks to Peabody Demonstration School—every one called it Peabody Dem—a private laboratory school just across the street from Peabody Teachers' College. Peabody Dem, red bricked and white columned, had a large well-tended playing field behind and many tennis courts on one side. The basement held a swimming pool, heated in the winter months. Most luxurious of all, when swimming class was over, we had a hair drying system involving a long pipe filled with warm air blowing from a row of holes. Swimmers sat on a bench in front of the pipe until our hair was dry, and on a winter's day, we were warm all over. I had no idea what my brother's school in Kittanning was like, although I suspected he wasn't happy there.

At long intervals my father went to Pennsylvania on leave to see Billy or came to Nashville to check on me. Twice in four years he brought my brother back with him.

"Look at them! They look like two little animals!" Miss Jones, our grandmother's nurse, stood above us talking to Annie.

Billy and I, rolling off the living room rug to the hardwood floor, were a tangled mass of arms and legs punching and kicking. Intent on our quarrel, we hadn't heard the two women approach. But when Miss Jones made her pronouncement, we instantly let go of each other and stood upright.

"We are not animals!" I said in a loud voice. I knew not to shout. Our grandmother was napping in the next room. So paralyzed she couldn't lift her head or speak, the only noise she could make was a strangled sounding cry coming from somewhere deep in her throat. She made it seldom and usually when in pain. I didn't want to cause that cry.

Annie retreated noiselessly to her kitchen.

What else I said exactly, I don't know; however, angry as I was at Miss Jones I managed to report to the nurse a number of complaints I'd heard my two aunts make against her including, "You try to make Grandmother eat olives and she doesn't like them."

Full of self-righteous indignation over anyone trying to make another person eat anything, I accused Miss Jones falsely. She fed Grandmother her supper at the family table every night, and in truth my aunts told me later, she'd offered the olives; she didn't "try to make" Grandmother eat them.

Billy had recently come from Pennsylvania for his first visit. He was an essentially active little boy who was always falling off a tree limb or slipping on the cellar steps where no one but Owen, the yardman, went to stoke the boiler, or banging his fingers with a hammer he happened to find on the back porch. And no matter how badly I wanted his company we fought a lot; he was a great tease and I reacted too readily. Worse, according to our childless aunts, he often ran away from school just as he'd run away from kindergarten in California when he was five and still in our mother's care. Because he'd arrived in Nashville in the middle of the year, we were in different schools. I had no idea why he continually ran away, nor did he ever let me know about his escape plans. Probably he had none; probably running away from school was his reaction to any sort of unhappiness. Now I think perhaps losing a mother when he was seven, even if he was assured he was loved, he couldn't accept our aunts as substitutes. He may have been more comfortable with our aunt and uncle in Pennsylvania since their home was the last place he'd seen our mother. Someone from his school would call, and then both Aunt Elnora and Aunt Dorothy, anxious about keeping their brother's children, had to drop everything at their jobs to search frantically for their nephew. They always found him in the neighborhood near the school. He didn't know his way home, and I slowly realized, he wanted to be found. Neither he nor our aunts said a word about his adventures on the streets. I was told only that Billy had run away again and he would be going back to Pennsylvania. Once my harried father arrived to take him; Uncle Gerald may have come to get him after his second visit. Billy never acted like he minded leaving.

"I like it better up there," he said and this was all he said. He was as tight-lipped as a little boy as he would be when he became a grown man.

For sassing the nurse, my aunts ordered me to apologize and to invite Miss Jones to go with me to see *The Student Prince*, an operetta playing in Nashville then. I didn't look forward to spending an evening with Miss Jones. She was personally as antiseptic as her always clean white uniform. Spare, almost devoid of personality, Miss Jones was, to me, a background figure. To my aunts she was foreground.

"Remember, she's Mama's registered nurse. We simply can't live without her." Aunt Elnora said.

"Where would we find another live-in nurse in wartime?" Aunt Dorothy asked. Both of them were always asking questions I wasn't supposed to answer.

Aunt Elnora taught school five days a week. Aunt Dorothy was a daily newspaper reporter. They had to work. To placate Miss Jones, I would have to take her by myself downtown at night in a taxi to the Ryman Auditorium, the venue of the operetta. My aunts trusted I would be as polite as possible.

The novelty of a taxi ride dismissed any vengeful feelings I might have been trying to suppress. Miss Jones and I both loved *The Student Prince*, especially when grown men standing on table-tops clanked beer steins and bellowed *The Drinking Song*, which I hummed all the way home in another splendid taxi.

After that Miss Jones faded to the background once more.

Whether from continual worry or from genetic mischance, both aunts had prematurely white hair. Aunt Elnora, dyed her own 1920s style bob black and used a curling iron heated on the kitchen stove's top to turn the ends under. I wanted to see her dye it, although I knew better than to say so because she locked the bathroom door and cleaned the sink so rigorously that not a bit of black showed. Although she taught home economics, she so detested cooking she would only go in the kitchen to heat her curling iron, or on her way to the garage, or to speak to Annie about what we were going to have for supper. She had a master's degree in home economics and taught eighth grade girls how to cook at a school in east Nashville. Years later I wondered if the scientific side may have interested her more. She could speak at length about amounts of protein and vitamins in certain foods, but she hardly ever spoke of her work.

When she came back from a first teaching job in Oklahoma and a tour to Europe shortly before the war began, she told me in the off-hand way older people will tell a child about huge chunks of their lives. "Papa wasn't well and Mama wasn't going to get any better. I knew I had to come home to help look after her." These were the days before my grandfather's last heart attack, before Miss Jones came to work. I wondered if Aunt Elnora simply got stuck in the job as well as in the classic role of maiden daughter.

Of the two aunts, she was the disciplinarian. I was never whipped or physically punished in any way;

instead Aunt Elnora gave me "a talking to." Unimpressed by this leniency, I reported to my father when he came home on leave, "I'd rather be whipped than listen to one of her sermons." Delivered in a patient-yet-determined voice, they involved ungratefulness, disobedience, bad manners, or any number of other misbehaviors. Though given infrequently, she always had one suitable for wrongdoing. I learned I was morally lacking in many ways but I tended to forget which ones.

"You mustn't complain about rice pudding again. Sugar is far too scarce to waste on special desserts for one person. And it's too much work. To make demands like that on Annie is selfish. I really can't imagine what you were thinking."

I thought, of course, that I would never like rice pudding. Annie continued to make it, and I continued to take a tiny bite before asking to be excused from the table quickly when it appeared.

Aunt Dorothy was more fun. During pre-war visits to our grandparents, she was the one who'd shown Billy and me how to play King of the Mountain by toppling one or the other of us off an old hassock, or letting us, when we were three and five, topple her. She was also the one who gave both of us practical joke toys, the ink bottle lying on its side with the super-realistic inky looking tin piece for instance. If we placed it correctly near a chair leg, we hoped to alarm an adult by crying, "Oh, you've turned over an ink bottle on the rug!" From the same store she brought the fascinating pill-sized snakes which, when lit, grew and curled resulting in such disgustingly smelly puffs of smoke we had to light them outside…with her supervision, of course.

At *The Tennessean*, Nashville's morning paper, she worked on the Society Desk, sometimes as an editor, sometimes as a reporter. After graduating from Vanderbilt—with a major in English—and working on *The Tennessean* for a short time, she'd gone to D.C. where she'd been offered a job at *Time* magazine but chose to marry and return to Nashville. When the Army Air Corps sent her husband, Fred, to help supply air shipments flown over the Himalayas from India to Chinese troops, she vowed his orders turned her hair white and she kept it white. Always on the lookout for drama, I silently wished I'd been there to see this transformation and just as silently wondered why Aunt Elnora had decided to dye her white hair while Aunt Dorothy revealed hers.

Upstairs between my aunts' bedrooms, I could see through Aunt Elnora's open door, a place as tidy as the hotel rooms we'd lived in at the first of the war. I was expected to be tidy as well. Dirty clothes and linens were sent to White Way Laundry, but Annie served as housekeeper as well as cook. One of the household rules was: Do Not Impose on the Help. We made our own beds; immediately after using it, each person washed out the big claw-footed bathtub, the only one in the house, and we picked up whatever we dropped.

"Go get your doll rags ready," Aunt Elnora would demand when she thought I should choose my clothes for school the next day, or on any occasion that required dressing up.

I'd do it even though I detested those words. There was something fault finding in the term "doll rags," an accusation against my being a small child who always had to be told to prepare for the next step. Aunt Elnora, bent on preparation, also taught me how to pack my suitcase.

Aunt Dorothy's door—as opposed to Aunt Elnora's—was generally closed; however, I'd peeped in long enough to know her clothes drooped in layers from chair backs and stockings dangled off the same chair's arms. Powder, brushes, jewelry, ashtrays, and hairpins were jumbled together on top of her dresser, and her bed, if made, was lumpy. Her messiness equaled Aunt Elnora's orderliness. Along with everyone else, Aunt Dorothy banished Annie from her room for unspecified intervals.

On a weekend visit to the Griswolds' house, Aunt Thelma, my mother's younger sister, tried to help me comb my long stringy blonde hair. She and Uncle Nelson had recently moved back to Nashville from Franklin. Their one son, Nelson, Jr., my only first cousin, had hair so curly I envied him. Envy also made me despise Shirley Temple because all the adults I knew thought her the perfectly darling curly-headed girl I was sure I would never be.

"What is this?" Aunt Thelma lifted the layer of hair

I'd so carefully combed over the tangled mat on the back of my head.

Sitting in front of her dresser's big mirror, I spoke to her reflection, "I tried, but it hurt too much to comb it."

"Well…" She pressed her lips together, left the room, and returned with a pair of scissors.

"I don't know what else to do."

The whacked off mass of hair fell in the wastebasket and the lank combed-over cover fell limply against my neck.

Aunt Thelma laughed. "Don't worry, honey. It'll grow back. I'll tell Elnora and Dorothy I cut it."

Afterward she showed me how to use a brush and from time to time, as I grew older, my aunts sent me to a nearby beauty parlor. Hooked up to a machine dangling black wires, a contraption I thought resembled Miss Muffet's giant spider, hovering over me, I got a series of disastrous permanents resulting in frizz which took forever to grow out to presentable curls. Having solved their own hair problems, my aunts determined they had solved mine as best they could.

On one of his visits, Billy solved his by asking me to cut off the hated curl that fell over his forehead. Like our mother, he had dark brown curly hair, which grown-ups casually ruffled when passing Pleased to oblige him, I used my pair of child-sized nickel-plated scissors, so dull it took three awkward cuts to remove the curl. And, of course, he tattled. Despite Aunt Thelma's good example, our aunts regarded the act with deep displeasure.

Of all the secrets in our family, the greatest one was my mother's condition. If I asked about her, one of the aunts said, "She's doing as well as can be expected." If my teachers or friends inquired, they cautioned me to give the same useless information. My fourth grade teacher was the only one who ever thought to ask the question. Though thankful for her interest, I could only mutter the rote answer. I sensed the lie, but how great a lie I told I couldn't know.

Then my father, on one of his leaves, came home so drunk he almost fell in the front door while the rest of us were eating supper.

Aunt Dorothy stood up, still clutching her napkin.

Aunt Elnora murmured, "Oh, Brother!" in a mournful voice.

He staggered upstairs to bed repeating; "I don't understand what's wrong with Katherine."

I hadn't heard him speak Mother's name for such a long time. He'd changed so strangely his warped character frightened me, and I began crying. In an effort to comfort me, my aunts told me he'd been to visit Mother; she had, by then, been moved to Central Tennessee State Mental Hospital on the outskirts of Nashville, and, no, her doctors still wouldn't allow her children to see her.

I had some familiarity with the old St. Thomas Hospital, the one where my brother and I were born.

A large red brick building near 1108, it stood in a neighborhood we sometimes drove through. But I had neither knowledge nor mental image of Central Tennessee State Mental Hospital. Almost a void, the place where my mother lived, grew into a forbidding amorphous shape out there somewhere on the edge of the city, just as she remained on the edge of my life. Somehow just knowing approximately where she was made her absence more bearable. As she had been before, she remained away; only now she had grown closer.

One birthday morning Aunt Dorothy woke me with a large illustrated edition of *Heidi* and for years to come, on any occasion, and sometimes only because I had to stay in bed with a bad cold, she gave me, among others, *The Secret Garden*, *Little Lord Fauntleroy*, *Five Little Peppers and How They Grew*, and a whole collection of books that began with *Miss Minerva and William Greenhill*, a book I read and reread. About a mischievous orphaned boy who suddenly had to go live with a maiden aunt, *William Greenhill*, preferably called *Billy* as my own brother was, must have been my fictional replacement for him. *Heidi, Five Little Peppers,* and all the other orphans—I identified with each one— were inexact images of myself. I also received a number of books about girls who were sent off to boarding schools, usually in Switzerland, where they were terribly unhappy until they adjusted.

My father wrote Aunt Dorothy, "I'm glad to know Carolyn is adjusting well." This was one of those comforting lies she'd told to her brother away in the army.

There was a lot to adjust to. No one tucked me in bed. Dark stairs led up to a landing; at a right angle, another shorter stairway led to the upstairs hall and everyone's bedroom. At nine o'clock on my way up, Hattie, the black night nurse, would have relieved Miss Jones and would be getting Grandmother ready for bed. Climbing the first set of stairs—the light only reached that far—I would pass Hattie's small bed in the screened alcove between the stairway and Grandmother's room. Hattie was better tempered than Annie and larger. Best of all, she had an easy buck-toothed smile. My father called her "Mrs. Roosevelt," which wasn't a disparagement; we all liked the Roosevelts. How I yearned for Hattie's reassuring presence in the empty dark alcove! No specific terrors waited in it or on the landing above, probably the cause of the vague yet certain fear I wouldn't admit. Babies were afraid of the dark.

"Go on," I told myself. "Just go on." I clattered up the stairs as fast as I could to the landing where a big window overlooked the dark back yard and the second light switch would be on my right when I turned to go up the last small flight of stairs.

Weekday mornings my aunts went to work early. Annie, never much of a talker, gave me breakfast at the large round dining table, a raft in an ocean of space. Generally still half asleep in the mornings, I drifted along happily. Sometimes I read parts of the rumpled

Tennessean Aunt Dorothy left at her place; mostly I day-dreamed.

— ⊷✦⊶ —

After breakfast I walked three blocks to Peabody Dem. Older students said our parents paid for us to serve as guinea pigs for would-be teachers, but this was only the self-mockery of the privileged. In truth a number of our teachers had PhD's, and practice teachers showed up only for short periods.

The public grammar schools I'd attended previously, the usual small factory-looking buildings, have faded from my memory, not because I was particularly awed by the grandeur of Peabody Dem; while there I saw it as part of our ordinary scenery. Before the war began we passed the campus every time we drove to my grandparents' house. Vanderbilt, Aunt Dorothy's university, was just across the street. Aunt Elnora and my mother's degrees were from Peabody. Both Aunt Dorothy and Aunt Elnora's high school degrees were from a girls' school nearby, Ward-Belmont, another Nashville institution.

At school, beside the usual subjects, we took music where, including other classics, we learned *The Hallelujah Chorus*, in preparation, I suppose, for attending a performance of *The Messiah* sponsored by the college. We were also given piano lessons on black and white paper keyboards. I had difficulty making the connection between hitting a paper key when the teacher hit the same key on a real piano. We had only one, so a student per class got to touch it. When it was my turn, I generally got too excited to hit the right key. During art lessons we wove coasters out of raffia in imitation of the baskets woven by Indians we were studying, a strange imitation, I felt, since the Indians had no glasses.

Peabody was so progressive we didn't receive report cards; instead we were given a sheet of paper with spaces drawn for subjects, and these spaces were filled with our teachers' hand-written assessments.

In spite of all the attention given to us by caring teachers in small classes, in spite of spacious, well-planned surroundings, in spite of my own interest in English and history particularly, I managed to be as miserable as any child who'd been shipped off to an elegant Swiss boarding school. Uprooted since the war began, I'd already been to a number of new schools where I was one of many army brats. At Peabody, I automatically became the stranger facing another tribe.

Edward, the biggest boy in the fourth grade, could have been called the chief. He bullied everyone. One day we were both standing in front of the blackboard: the teacher being momentarily out of class, he punched my arm. I turned and socked him in his stomach. I hadn't known I was going to fight back; I simply reacted. Edward was so surprised he left me alone afterward, but everyone else still did the same. The usual children's insult—being the last one chosen for any team—remained my fate. The four girls I'd determined I wanted as friends let me follow them around until they decided to gang up on the playground and pull off my cap. I caught colds frequently, and the aunts had made me promise to wear one. The girls tossed the wretched cap around while I chased after, one of many small humiliations that taught me how to pretend indifference. Some days I went home so angry I couldn't wait for the aunts to come home from work to tell them my troubles, so I took all my rolled up socks out of a drawer and threw them as hard and fast as I could, pair by pair, across the room. I knew I had to pick them up—Do Not Impose on the Help—but it felt good to throw them.

Aunt Dorothy reminded me, "Those children have been going to school together, most of them, since the first grade."

"The new ones always get picked on." Aunt Elnora, with her years of experience with school children's behavior, sighed while affirming the fact.

They realized, I think, their sympathy wasn't enough help, so they gave me a puppy, a fox terrier named Skippy I had to learn how to house-train, a responsibility I failed at first. I'd never known dogs had so much pee in them. Many puddles on the rugs and many clean-ups afterward, he began to keep me company sitting beside my desk while I did homework. However there was only so much homework to be done, only so many dog walks to take before Skippy disappeared for good. I looked for days, grieving while searching, before giving up. No other puppy was offered; runaways weren't favored at 1108. There were only so many ways to rearrange furniture in the dollhouse which, like me, lacked a family. Sometimes I wondered why no one made small dolls to fit it. I had to imagine miniature people moving around the little rooms. Altogether too wispy to endure long, they soon faded. For my ninth birthday while we were in Kittanning, my mother bought me a doll, yet even as I selected it, I'd known I'd outgrown dolls. Interest in them faded along with other fantasies such as dogs holding conversations when human were out of sight and a Santa Claus that came down the chimney. Our front yard, though filled with maples, was tiny, and in the back there was only the birdbath, the garage, and the closed slanting cellar doors where someone delivered coal by the truckload. I planted a victory garden nearby one spring. Nothing came up except some wan looking radishes and a Minié ball—identified by one of my aunts—buried in the dirt since the Battle of Nashville during the Civil War, an irony that escaped me at the time.

Annie told me early, "Stay out of my kitchen." At night when she was gone, I sometimes mixed anything I could find—cornmeal, flour, soda, baking powder, peanut butter, water—and put it in the oven half-hoping it would explode, but it never did. Why my aunts allowed me to do this, I don't know. Perhaps they indulged my whims for kitchen messes in hopes I'd become a cook. They remained in the living room while I stirred my potions and came in the kitchen only to see if I'd washed every reliably sticky dish and wiped the table clean. After a winter evening or two, I gave up kitchen entertainment.

Outside I could walk almost to the bottom of Eighteenth Avenue and up to the top of its hill. Of course when I was ten and got a bike, my territory expanded a block or two away where I could pick up medicine for Grandmother at the drugstore, such an important errand, I never lingered a moment. This was the only unusual distance allowed as the aunts' anxieties kept me close. While housebound I read anything available, including volumes of Grandmother's leather-bound historical romances; I generally skipped the history in order to get on with the romance. Though there were no forbidden books in the house, I thought *Gone With the Wind* might be. I doubled an imaginary forbidden pleasure by using a flashlight and reading under the bedcovers.

Aunt Dorothy, coming in late from the newspaper one night, stood at my door and asked, "What are you doing in your tent?"

"Reading."

"What?"

I gave up. "*Gone With the Wind.*"

"Well, let it go till tomorrow. You'll hurt your eyes in such weak light."

Once discovered, half the pleasure of reading a presumed forbidden book vanished. I finished *Gone With the Wind* in several afternoons.

Soon after I moved in, the aunts took some of my parents' furniture out of storage to furnish my bedroom, which made it more familiar; I slept in the sleigh bed that my parents had slept in, saw myself in the mirror of my mother's dresser. The only truly strange object in the room was on the mantelpiece, a smiling ceramic blonde head of a man with an upturned curled mustache. On his head he wore a removable pink fez. My grandfather had kept some of his tobacco in the hollow beneath the fez. The man's brilliant dark eyes stared straight at me over the foot of the bed. Every night I turned his head to the wall and every morning I turned him around again. This became as habitual as waking to watch the squirrels playing in the maple tree branches outside the double front windows.

Eventually one of Aunt Dorothy's friends took refuge at her father's house across the street for the remainder of the war. She had two children, an older boy, Sandy, and a daughter, Elizabeth, about my age. Like my father, theirs was in the army. Together we discovered Janie and Phillip living in an apartment nearby. Their mother brought them to Nashville from New Orleans to live near relatives while their father was away in the army. We all went to different schools, but the loneliness of after school hours lifted.

During the gray winter days lasting from November through February the house could be gloomy. "Mouse days," Aunt Dorothy called them because, she said, they were as gray as mice and just as plentiful. My grandparents had furnished their house sparsely with ornately carved golden oak in the bedrooms; in the living room they had accumulated a sofa, two chairs, a hassock, two lamps, an upright Steinway piano Aunt Elnora seldom played, and a wind-up Victrola no one touched although Aunt Dorothy gave me a demonstration of the way it worked; she cranked the handle and a tin looking record with holes in it miraculously allowed Caruso to sing. I wanted to play some more but Aunt Dorothy warned me away as the mechanism had almost worn out. At the distant end of the room we ate all our meals at the round, black table surrounded by six straight chairs that creaked when you sat down and again when you got up. At the house we'd lived in before the war, we shared a cheerful yellow breakfast nook my father built. Why was the dining room table so dark?

Aunt Elnora, in a rather disdainful voice, said the table was "that old fumed oak," fumed with ammonia to make it dark like the mission style furniture popular when my grandparents moved into their house. This was my introduction to various styles; until I lived at 1108, furniture was just furniture.

Radiators, connected by pipes to a boiler in the basement, pinged and sighed while heating the house. Installed by my grandfather, the system became a reminder of his father, an Irish immigrant who'd apprenticed himself to learn boiler making and passed the trade on to his son.

My front bedroom upstairs had been the one Grandfather stayed in alone after Grandmother became ill. He'd died in that room, a seemingly morose atmosphere for a child, however my memory of him as a benign person must have prevented any fears I might have had. Rotund, balding, half deaf, sometimes impish, he'd encouraged my curiosity when we visited on Sundays before the war. I wanted to know what his chewing tobacco tasted like.

He pointed to the large twisted brown rope and said, "Try it."

I chomped a bite from the rope and ran out to the front porch to spit it in the yard while my aunts and parents remonstrated with him.

"But she wanted to know," he kept saying and laughing until we all laughed with him.

He taught me to sing a simple little song that began, "Sunday school is over and we are going home." We shouted the chorus together. "Goodbye now. Goodbye now, for we are going home." Apparently he enjoyed the shouting part as much as I did. Once during those pre-war visits he'd taken Billy upstairs to his room and taught him how to strike matches, much to my parents' disapproval.

"Striking matches is men's business," he said and refused to teach me.

That was the only time he'd made me unhappy.

I thought people naturally died at home in their beds. My aunts fully expected Grandmother to die in hers. The knowledge of her suffering saddened them, though they didn't speak of it often and they did everything they could to relieve her. She had an always clean, always neat, mass of white hair and startling blue eyes. Miss Jones bathed her and kept her in immaculate soft dresses. Even if her head fell to one side and she couldn't sit up straight, even though she was mute except for the one cry she could make, she seemed to recognize people. In her lap there was always a box of tissues. When her paralysis overcame the ability to control her saliva and it ran down her chin, the person nearest her wiped her mouth. Much aware of Grandmother's housebound life, my aunts, on some days after work, no matter how tired they were, and on nearly every weekend, would lift her into a straight chair with long poles attached to either side. Bearing her coolie fashion, they carried her outside, and in a series of careful movements, slid her into the front seat of Aunt Dorothy's sedan. Nobody mentioned gasoline rationing; a drive, to my aunts, was so soothing it was a medical necessity.

On Sundays, with Grandmother in the car, we often visited Mt. Olivet Cemetery where my grandfather and other family members were buried. Aunt Dorothy gave me family history lessons, and Aunt Elnora joined in to tell stories about the ones she'd known. Otherwise I was free to ramble around the ornate angels, the copy of Napoleon's tomb, another pyramid-shaped tomb complete with recumbent sphinxes, and to read Victorian verses carved in headstones. To my aunts, there was nothing morbid about visiting the cemetery. In this customary part of their lives, the dead were honored as part of a shared past.

Few men entered our house full of women. Formal pictures of my grandfather in a suit, of Uncle Fred in his Air Corps dress uniform, of my father in his Army dress uniform looked down from the top bookshelf in the living room. My father's leaves were infrequent; the army didn't allow many and some were dedicated to my brother. Grandfather had died, and Uncle Fred's post in India was, of course, too far away for home leave.

Other than Grandmother's doctor, who I once overheard briefly when he conferred with my aunts, I heard only the scary, gruff voice of Aunt Dorothy's father-in-law on the phone—he never visited—and the quiet "Yes, ma'am's" of the black yardman, Owen, who came inside to the back porch, or went through the kitchen to the cellar stairs so he could shovel coal in the boiler when the weather cooled. Uncle Ben, one of Grandfather's relatives, a small shrunken man— ancient, I thought, somewhere in his eighties—showed up at Sunday dinner about twice a year. Occasionally Jack, Aunt Elnora's alcoholic boyfriend, who the rest of the family adamantly disliked, visited. He'd had a brief career as a tennis player and a country club tennis coach before volunteering for the army. He didn't serve long, for reasons Aunt Elnora wouldn't discuss. He worked at the downtown post office and lived with his mother. A collection of silver looking cups he'd won in tennis tournaments shone on the small table under a tall mirror just beside the front door. Annie must have polished them for they reflected light grandly. Since Aunt Elnora governed the house, I guessed the display of his gifts to her had to be allowed.

I didn't actively dislike Jack. He had a long, always tan, beseeching face, making him look as if you knew the answer to something he needed to know. His hair was so precisely combed and slicked, I thought he could have rolled a dime down the part. Tall and lean, he would have looked good dressed in tennis whites. Unfortunately stooped shoulders marred his appearance. Although he gave me a few tennis lessons at the Peabody Dem. courts two or three Saturdays, I felt his heart couldn't be in his coaching; Aunt Elnora waited invisibly behind him. One evening early I walked in on the dismaying scene of Jack weeping on my aunt's shoulder and by the unhappy look on her face, I knew he was drunk at the time. Afterward I felt uneasy around him. He wasn't a dependable sort of grown up.

On some weekends when I was ten or eleven, one of the aunts walked with me to the bus stop to ride the eighteen miles to Franklin to visit my mother's family, or Aunt Elnora would drive me out to stay with my cousin my age; Mary Anne lived with her two brothers and parents just outside the city's limits. If I was in Nashville, I had to attend Sunday school at Belmont Methodist Church, one my grandparents had helped organize. On my way there I walked over the Peabody College campus kicking small stones and anything else in my path. At home Aunt Dorothy would be sleeping late; perhaps Aunt Elnora went back to bed once I was gone. Why they had to have so much sleep and why I had to represent the family by showing up at Sunday school, I couldn't understand. Reading through old letters years after I found my father's orders: "Tell Carolyn she is to go to Sunday school regularly." Usually my aunts' requirements were not unjust. Their paramount rule was: Do Not Make Noise. This got in the way when I finally, after all of the fourth grade and half of the fifth, made friends enough to create a club with the four girls I liked best. They had known each other since first grade, but I was the only one who lived in a house near school. One game, among others we created, required jumping on the living room sofa. Either Annie or Miss Jones tattled resulting in a "talking to," the one called Do Not Disturb Your Grandmother's Rest, sub-titled, Selfishness Will Not Be Tolerated. I felt quite low after this. It hadn't been my idea to jump on the sofa, but, as Aunt Elnora said, I didn't tell anyone else not to either. This clubby stage extended across the street to Elizabeth's grandfather's old barn, which had become her family's garage. Steps on one wall outside led upstairs to a small empty room with one window. With Janie we diligently cleaned away the cobwebs and dust, but once clean, we didn't know what to do with our clubroom except to deny entrance to any interested boys. Elizabeth's brother, Sandy, and Janie's brother, Phillip, were woefully uninterested. While it was still warm enough to be outside, we moved to a large many-branched tree in Elizabeth's backyard. Each of us claimed a fork where we could sit and read in the afternoons.

One Saturday Elizabeth whispered, "There's that man again."

We looked up from our books to see a fully clothed man at a neighboring second story window overlooking our tree.

"What's he doing?" I asked

Janie said, "The usual…. Nothing, just staring."

We all stared at him for a little until Elizabeth suggested, "Let's wave at him."

Janie and I both refused. Neither one of us questioned why we felt uncomfortable at the thought.

When I told my aunts about the man standing staring through the window at us, they only looked at each other. Before the following Saturday, however, a new rule was made: Do Not Read In Trees. We could too easily fall out and break a leg, the only explanation the two mothers and my aunts would give. We didn't particularly mind since the weather soon changed and it was too cool to sit in a tree and read.

In those female-dominated years, we were still curious about sex. We asked each other questions, but no one knew an answer about the main one, "Where do babies come from?"

"Navels," because no one knew what they were for, remained the most popular answer though no one thought it made any sense.

What about boys and their *tallywhackers*, the only word we knew for that part of the male anatomy. I'd picked it up somewhere, perhaps from my father, and never repeated it to my aunts. Or perhaps I'd overheard Aunt Lorene's husband, Uncle Frank, father to my country cousin, talking to his two sons. During one of my visits, Mary Anne and I found her father's condoms in the bathroom. We didn't know their name or their purpose, but instinctively we knew these stretchy things had to do with *tallywhackers*. Wondering how they looked when worn, we stuffed a condom as full of cotton as possible and after considering its length, decided I should take "the snake" home.

Whatever caused this decision we forgot about it until Aunt Elnora, who had come to pick me up, checked through my suitcase just before we left Mary Anne's.

The sight of my maiden aunt pulling the cotton-stuffed condom out of my suitcase sent us into barely repressed giggles, but the frowns on Aunt Lorene's and Aunt Elnora's faces silenced us.

"What is this?" Aunt Elnora asked.

"Um...I don't know," I said truthfully.

"Me neither," said Mary Anne.

"Well, how did it get in here?" Aunt Elnora, as usual, had to get to the bottom of a question.

"I don't know," I lied.

Aunt Lorene relieved my aunt of "the snake" and tried to stuff it in her apron pocket.

Seeing it dangling between them, Mary Anne and I crossed our arms over our stomachs to keep from laughing. We couldn't look at each other since we both sensed if we did we wouldn't be able to contain ourselves a minute longer.

On the way home, the silence between Aunt Elnora and me in the front seat of the Pontiac grew so dreadful I fell into a fit of non-stop crying over my sins. Before going to bed that night I confessed I'd lied. Instead of receiving a "talking to," shortly after this incident Aunt Dorothy casually handed me a small book where the way babies were born was explained in simple language.

"If you've got any questions, you can ask me," she offered.

Embarrassed by my ignorance, I shook my head, so I had to wait a while longer to learn what the stretchy things were.

⋯⋯⋯⋯

Time crept on. I could see the hours slow passing on the watch my father mailed me from the post's PX one Christmas. I'd asked for a little WAC uniform in emulation of his military splendor. Neither he nor my aunts saw fit to honor such a wish. I thought Mother would have if she'd been well, but she wasn't. I missed her sharply during the year's holidays just as I missed my father and brother. These intermittent aches were gradually calmed by the recurrent panacea of dailiness, sometimes dull but generally reassuring. Billy continued to stay in Pennsylvania with our aunt and uncle. Aunt Allie would write to me occasionally and enclose comic strips she'd cut out of the paper. I couldn't imagine my brother's life as she sent little or no news of him; instead her letters were full of moralistic pieties about how I should bear up, be good, love everybody, and pray incessantly. I had a shirt-pocket brass-covered copy of the *New Testament*, the kind that reputedly saved a soldier by stopping the bullet meant for his heart, just the thing for someone whose father was in the army. I'd read it through, said my prayers every night, and did double duty by going to Sunday school as well as to church when my aunts elected to attend. Because Aunt Allie assumed I was in want of her constant admonitions, her letters so depressed me I had a hard time bearing up. The sight of her handwriting on an envelope could drive me to tears. For weeks I collected the detested letters unopened in my dresser drawer. In a forbearing mood, I would open a bunch all at once, read the comic strips we didn't get in the Nashville papers, and throw the letters away. My Methodist aunts knew my reaction; they also knew Aunt Allie's reputation for religious extremism. After I'd read them parts of a letter or two, they may have been affronted by her apparent belief that they were failing in my religious education. Neither one of them ever suggested I stop trashing those letters.

I wondered how Billy could bear up under so much of Aunt Allie's scolding. I wanted to think he ignored it. He was good at that.

To relieve our ordinary schedules, and to get our minds off the war, my aunts took me, at what seemed like long intervals, to a shop called Candyland that offered ice-cream sodas and concoctions such as "Hay Stack Sundaes." Aunt Elnora's favorite bakery in a shopping center near the house was The Cupboard and it contained chocolate éclairs we carried home for dessert if we could wait that long. Aunt Dorothy and I once devoured the bakery's last éclairs and took Aunt Elnora a cream puff. No explanations about how sugar rationing affected The Cupboard's supply of preferred pastry excused us. For our greed, we suffered a severe "talking to."

One aunt or the other would accompany me to children's theatre productions. I went to innumerable music recitals including Aunt Elnora's favorite, Alec Templeton, the blind pianist, and to the *Ballet Russe de Monte Carlo* whenever it appeared in Nashville. My aunts' cultural interests didn't extend to the *Grand Old Opry*. Even if Aunt Dorothy knew the lady who played Minnie Pearl, they were unrepentant in their choices: country music was, to them, for country people who came to town to hear it on Saturday nights. Of the other music I heard, the most stirring was the *Don Cossack Chorus.* All those male voices as well as our wartime alliance with Russia made them enormously popular. Their formidable ability to thrust straight forward a long boot-covered leg while in a kneeling position and holding their crossed arms in front led me, in hopeless imitation, to topple over often on hard ground in the backyard. Once I tried balancing myself against the garage wall, but that didn't work either.

We toured Andrew Jackson's Hermitage once. Through its ancient windows in the back we could see the slave headquarters. We didn't go outside to see them. I don't really know why not. Aware of prejudice though they were southerners—the "n" word was forbidden as "white-trash" usage—I can't say they were particularly liberal about race. As educated white women, they used the words "colored" or "Negro."

Often, as it was closer, we went to Centennial Park to view Nashville's full-scale copy of Athens's Parthenon, built for Tennessee's centennial celebration of statehood in 1896. There was nothing much inside in the 1940s except an occasional art show and the basement's replicas of the original statues on the building's pediments.

"Lord Elgin's marbles," my aunts murmured in tones reserved for a revered past. I didn't know who Lord Elgin was, or why it was so important whether he'd stolen or merely saved the original marble figures from destruction in Greece. All that had to be discovered in the future. When I was first introduced to the dusty gray plaster copies I asked, "Why are they naked?"

"Because they are gods," Aunt Dorothy said.

"Yes," Aunt Elnora agreed and hurried us on out to the lake in front so I could feed the ducks, something my aunts considered a treat, but I didn't. Ducks were tiresomely predictable. You threw; they ate. Naked gods were much more interesting, but I understood the subject couldn't be repeated.

Though I liked walking over the little high-arched bridge in the Japanese garden, for patriotic reasons, I didn't ask to go there. As no one else did either, the city allowed it to be neglected. Other than the gradual disappearance of the garden and a horrifying poster of a Japanese soldier—with buckteeth, a bayonet, and a baby speared on the end of it—at the grocery store, I didn't see many memorable visual signs of propaganda. Because I had a soldier father and a tendency to wake my aunts with screaming nightmares of threatening Nazis—I'd seen them in their swastika marked black uniforms in newspaper pictures— I was not allowed to go to war movies. In fact the only movies allowed were Saturday afternoon matinees to see *Fantasia* and a few black and white serial episodes when visiting my grandmother in Franklin.

The tedium of winter in Nashville changed the year we had deep snow. Much of the traffic stopped, schools closed, and all the children in our neighborhood tried to slide down Eighteenth Avenue's hill. In a southern city where big snowfalls were infrequent, cardboard took the place of sleds. I ran to Annie who grudgingly loaned me a pie pan to try, a rather unsatisfactory eight inch round piece of aluminum. The snowman we built turned out better. We'd all seen pictures in children's books and knew exactly what was needed for the snowman's face; a carrot for a nose, small broken sticks for a mouth, a top hat no one could find, and two pieces of coal for his eyes. There was plenty of coal to be had since Nashville burned soft coal for heat and energy. Not until after the war did a gas pipeline reach our sooty city. The heavy snowfall gave us a day's blessed relief. Once our everyday darkness had miraculously disappeared, it seemed our whole world had been washed clean.

By the next day, the customary soot filmed over our melting snowman, grimed the white covered yards. We were used to it, breathed it every day, watched it gray the wallpaper in our houses, but the way it covered the whiteness was as dispiriting as the war news.

Though war movies were out, the war's reality came to us in the newspaper and over the radio. On certain nights, with the help of Hattie, my aunts carried Grandmother to the sofa so she could have a change from her wheelchair. They took the living room chairs, I sat on the hassock, and a coal fire burned quietly in the grate while we listened to Walter Winchell blurting out the war news. His staccato delivery made it all sound bad. After the bombing of Pearl Harbor, other than knowing our chief enemies were the Germans and the Japanese, until I was twelve and began earnestly reading the paper, I had no real understanding of the war. I knew none of the particular advances or retreats nor could I have named even the most famous battles. To me it was a vast and terrible confusion that had already hospitalized my mother, divided my brother and me, and threatened to kill my father and my uncle.

In fact I objected to taking ballroom dancing lessons because I couldn't see any reason for dancing during a war, or so I said. Actually I dreaded any project involving dancing with boys. Aunt Dorothy's friend, "Hank" Fort, had begun collecting a class of children my age, which would meet every two weeks called "Fortnightly."

I told my aunt, "I don't want to get all dressed up and go learn how to dance while there's a war on."

"Honey, learning how to dance isn't going to hurt the war effort," said Aunt Dorothy. She continued, "Just try it, and if you don't like it, you don't have to go back."

In a new dress—light blue with maroon smocking—wearing black patent leather Sunday shoes and white socks, I approached dancing with my dread decently clothed. The class met in a slightly shabby two-story mansion containing a ballroom covered by mirrors on one side, the same room my mother had sent me to for ballet lessons the year before the war when I was six. "Hank," a gray-haired, friendly woman who expected even her students to call her by her nickname welcomed us. No taller than most of her students, constantly laughing, she was like a slightly older sister first teaching us to enjoy the random pairing of a Paul Jones, girls in one circle holding hands and moving clockwise, boys moving counter-clockwise in another, stopping to face each other only when the music stopped. She was so enthusiastic everyone, even the boys, forgot to be shy. They might have been as afraid of putting their arms around girls, as we feared touching them, however all our fears were soon danced away. By the time our first lesson finished, I was ready to return to "Fortnightly." Hank had showed us the special way of holding and moving with each other to music—supplied by a nearly invisible woman hidden by the open top of a grand piano. Together, in later classes, we learned the box waltz and the two-step Hank called "The St. Louis Shuffle," and other basics such as filling out a dance cards, a formality most of us would never need to know except for her classes. Though bombs fell and people shot each other on the opposite side of the world, the women on this side went on training the next generation.

A two-week Girl Scout Camp, located next to a lake at Montgomery Bell Park, was another place I didn't particularly want to go. Finally I went because swimming lessons were promised. These lessons ended with an instructor holding a long pole just in front of me while I took the first Red Cross test. Relieved I had no need to grab the pole, I found I could trust myself in deep water. I also learned how to get along with five other strange girls my age in the same cabin, how not to gripe about latrine duty, and freckles appeared when you spent days in the sun. The aunts offered me another two weeks, but I wanted to come home. In reality I was a little hurt they thought to offer. I missed them, missed sitting on the porch every night and waiting for the upstairs bedrooms to get cool enough for sleeping. These were the hours my aunts relaxed after their day's work, the time they talked in an easy, desultory way. Stretched out on the glider, I listened to memories of their pasts, to daily incidents, and to family stories.

A new audience for these, I heard stories not told to deliberately entertain; rather they were interwoven in their conversation.

"I'd like to go to Ireland someday," Aunt Dorothy would say.

"Our grandfather's ship from Ireland landed in Charleston." Aunt Elnora said.

Aunt Dorothy went on, "In 1849. After he got there he used to sit on a dock waiting for the latest installment of one of Charles Dickens's novels. They ran in the newspapers, you know, and those papers would arrive on a boat from England."

"He had a brother who came with him, didn't he?"

Aunt Elnora picked up the thread again. "Yes. I wish I could remember his first name. He left for California. Forty-nine was the gold rush year, you know. But we don't know if he made it or not. That's why I look in phone books and call up people named Culbert whenever I'm in a strange city."

I wanted to know if she ever found any clues to our missing great uncle, but conversation moved on. There were many unfinished stories.

After I came back to 1108 from scout camp that summer, Aunt Dorothy taught me how to ride horseback English style on the broad leafy trails of Percy Warner Park. I had already begun to learn how to ride western style on a bad-tempered Shetland pony at my other grandparents' farm on prewar visits. The horses for rent at the park's livery stable were mostly old reliables with names like Pokey. Aunt Dorothy taught by example and warning.

"Hold your reins this way." She wove her fingers in and out of the four narrow strips of leather.

"Post like this." She rose slightly from the saddle and sat down again, then off she trotted saying, "Heels down, back straight."

Pokey waited patiently until I finally remembered to flick the ends of the reins on his hide. We plodded after Aunt Dorothy's horse.

"Don't let him run back to the stable," my aunt directed. "Remember you are in charge."

She could claim that as long as she pleased. Pokey knew otherwise. He returned to the stable at a brisk trot with me wobbling in the saddle. It took longer to learn how to sit easily in an English saddle than it took to learn how to swim or to dance.

It seemed to take longer and longer for the war to be over. My father came home on leave and walked me to school wearing his full dress uniform, the pinks and greens, with the eagle flashing on his hat and the sun glancing off his polished brass insignia. I felt he was only a little less than God, and perhaps he would come to my class and meet my teacher, but no, he left me at the school's massive front door to go about business of his own—to see my mother, I suspected.

While he was home, Aunt Dorothy insisted we go to her newspaper's office where one of her photographer friends would take our picture. Our picture shows him seated with an expression on his face of a man who is finally humoring someone. I stand beside him, one hand on his shoulder as if by sheer will, I might keep him there. I could never look at that photograph without thinking about the two of us missing the other half of our family.

For the occasion my aunts had allowed me to wear a plaid lined coat with a shockingly different plaid skirt. In the years to come, I realized they over-looked such niceties. Whenever we went shopping for new clothes, they selected their favorite colors. My opinion wasn't asked.

"Don't you just love red?" Aunt Dorothy would say to the sales clerk.

"I prefer blue," said Aunt Elnora to another clerk another time.

It was always clear which one had taken me shopping by the predominant color of my clothes. My plaid skirt and plaid lined coat were both mainly red, so Aunt Dorothy chose them.

War's end, VJ Day, in 1945 surprised us early one night when church bells began ringing all over town. Aunt Dorothy, Aunt Elnora, Mary Anne, my cousin there for the weekend, and I all jumped into the Pontiac. Mary Anne and I got to take the rumble seat. We headed for Nashville's main street, Church Street, already clogged with people shouting, flinging their arms in the air, and hugging each other. The night was so filled with joy I was nearly dizzy at the sight. In a corner of a department store's side entrance a group of people threw their heads back and drank straight out of bottles of whisky.

In downtown Nashville a law forbade horn honking; that night everyone broke the law. We could hardly get through the street. At one intersection a soldier, bourbon bottle clutched in one extended arm, directed traffic. When we came along, he decided to sit down on the Pontiac's hood. Speared by its ornament, a shiny chrome Indian head with feathers, he jumped off, decapitating the Indian as he went.

I regretted losing the Indian's head, but Aunt Elnora said, "It doesn't matter. The war's over."

The destructive power of the atom bombs falling on Hiroshima and Nagasaki, the full scale of Nazi atrocities, I learned about later. Peace descended slowly. Uncle Fred returned and went through a long convalescence from the effects of various fevers. My father didn't part from the army until 1946. Late that summer he told me about my mother. We were driving out of Nashville to collect my brother, still in Pennsylvania.

"The doctors say she can't get well. She has something…they think it may be…they call it schizophrenia." He had a hard time saying the word.

I put my head down on the car's scratchy woolen seat cover and cried. It was a long time before I understood her form of mental illness but I knew immediately he had, at last, voiced the one thing I was most afraid of hearing. My father patted me on the back. Then he added that the chief of the psychiatric unit at Vanderbilt had told him to give up hoping for a cure.

"Don't worry. You won't get it," he said. I had no idea whether or not such illnesses could be inherited. You caught colds, or the measles, or chicken pox and you got over them. I didn't understand why schizophrenia couldn't be cured.

While my head was still on the seat, he told me he was going to marry again and our disbanded family would gather once more at my new mother's home, a little town in Texas. Somehow this didn't surprise me. I knew he liked Texas; there had been snippets of talk about someone he'd met there. And everything was changing then. Some of my friends' fathers had come back and taken them away to other places. I had a thousand questions to ask about this new mother, about the town she lived in, about all the uncertain future. There was only one certainty; the long years with the aunts were over. We all had a new set of adjustments to make.

III.

Going to Texas

Nearly a year after World War II was over and just before school started, my ten-year-old brother and I, twelve then, my father and his new wife—all of us nearly strangers to each other—piled in her bulky green Buick in Nashville one morning and drove west. We were on our way to a small town in central Texas called Gatesville. Crossing the Mississippi River, putting my head out the window to stare at its broad muddy width, the last boundary of my well-known southern world, I left Tennessee.

Of all the journeys I've taken, the trip that made the greatest difference to my life was the one moving us to Texas in the sliver of time between the atomic end of World War II and the beginning of the Korean War. Like many others, when the long awaited peace arrived my life was completely rearranged.

The only Texan in the car was our new mother, Mabel Winters Culbert. Married earlier that month, she'd been introduced to my father by mutual friends when he was stationed at South Ft. Hood just outside Gatesville.

Before we left, Billy and I didn't see our natural mother, diagnosed as incurably ill with schizophrenia. Our father, our grandmother Truett, our aunts and uncles could see her, but we were forbidden. Following medical trends in the forties, her doctors had ruled it would not help the patient, or her children, to see each other. No matter how often we begged, Billy and I were not allowed to go to Tennessee's Central State Mental Hospital on the outskirts of Nashville. To avoid passing on the stigma of mental illness in the family, all the adults apparently agreed we would be best protected by silence. This secrecy permeated our lives. As little was explained, we understood little. Neither my brother nor I had seen any manifestation of her illness. She was taken to the hospital when she attempted suicide, a fact we didn't know until we were adults. We were at a birthday party; when we came home, she was gone. Not until I was grown with children of my own would I see my mother again. At twelve her schizophrenia simply meant grief, a slow trickling kind of grief when I suspected she might not get well, followed by tears and more grief when I learned she could not.

Our father, a Colonel in the field artillery, released from the army at last but still active in the reserve in 1946, and I had already driven to Pennsylvania to reclaim Billy.

Except for two brief visits, we had been only children for three years; now together again, we hardly knew what to say to each other. I was deposited in Nashville with my aunts and grandmother once more while my brother went with our father to Lake Mead, Nevada, a place where they could both fish and get to know each other again. To my father being outdoors gave him both pleasure and comfort, for he found the natural world a consolation, one he meant to pass on to his son. After establishing residency in Nevada for six weeks, he obtained a divorce—at that time insanity wasn't one of the legal causes for divorce in Tennessee. On their way back to Nashville, they detoured to Texas to introduce Billy to our stepmother-to-be before my father returned to marry her. When I think of him driving us in a little black used La Salle coupe, the only car he could afford, all over the country that summer, I realize his desire to put his family back together was driving him.

How other people who've known real sorrow begin again, I'm not certain, however hope must have been traveling with us along with my own daily wonder at the new turns our lives were taking. Only a few days before leaving Nashville my father arrived with my new stepmother in her Buick. I waited on the front porch with my brother and aunts to meet her.

"What should I call her?" I asked when she'd gone upstairs while my father unloaded their luggage. My brother had the same problem even though he didn't say anything about it.

"Go and ask her," my aunts said.

I went immediately to my father's childhood bedroom where she was sitting at the dressing table after

*Mabel Winters Culbert, the wonderful second mother,
at her ranch, early 1940s.*

taking off her hat. Red felt, shaped like an upturned bucket with a bow around it, I thought it was a funny looking hat, but my aunts had admired it when they met her.

"So stylish," they murmured.

She also wore something called a snood, a heavy black web low on her head capturing her dark hair in back. Would she take that off too?

She didn't.

"What would you like for me to call you?" I let the question go in one breath.

"Mother," she said and smiled though there were tears in her eyes as well as mine.

Perhaps because she had no other children, after the first awkward, tearful moments, I began getting accustomed to saying it. Any fear I might have had about the wicked stepmothers I'd met in fairytales dissolved almost immediately. How children decide to like an absolutely new person so quickly, I don't know, but I think it must have to do partially with voice and touch as well as by words and need. Instinct propelled me. Eventually I came to believe I was lucky to have two good mothers. But at first, the four of us were like new leaves on a tree breaking into bud, making room for each other as they grew. In the car my brother and I sat far apart on the back seat, and when I moved up front so he could sleep, was it all right for me to put my head on Mother's lap to take a nap?

All the physical questions of touch and even taste had to be answered. None of us knew what anyone else usually ate, or exactly what time children or grown-ups generally went to bed, or even everyone's small personal habits like how many times a day we brushed our teeth. Because I wore braces, I was supposed to brush after every meal if possible, a duty I happily overlooked while traveling. My brother, for some reason, had never learned to hold a knife properly; no one said anything about his table manners. We made our way cautiously as we drove through one state, then another.

Before our natural mother's illness, we'd been as far north as Pennsylvania, through most of Tennessee and part of Arkansas after the war began, and we'd already driven across Oklahoma and the desert western states to reach our father's army post in California before returning to Tennessee in 1942. Our father was transferred to Ft. Hood much later in the war. I was lamentably ignorant about Texas. Western mythology hadn't penetrated my family already deeply absorbed in its own southern myths. Family and state history were passed on in stories I came to know as well as I knew the tastes of country ham and chess pie. But that was truer on my father's side. On my natural mother's side they were more occupied by the present. Perhaps because I visited them less, they had less inclination to tell me their stories. My maternal grandmother lived in her old Victorian duplex in Franklin after living in an older rose-red brick antebellum house out in the country nearby. She knew as well as everybody else the location of the house where after the Battle of Franklin, "five Confederate Generals were laid out dead on the porch," a phrase often repeated in the same words by others, but she wasn't especially interested in history—Confederate, family, or otherwise.

What I knew of Texas I'd seen in two or three Saturday afternoon serials in Franklin when visiting my grandmother. These involved riders wearing cowboy hats, sometimes also wearing bandannas tied just above their noses, galloping off to shoot—why I never discovered—or to save somebody, usually a woman. During the war my aunts thought I should be protected from its horrors. I suppose they believed the Civil War including the Battles of Nashville and Franklin with its five dead generals had receded to the safe historical past. As distant as the generals were, my aunts still insisted on keeping me from seeing the Saturday matinees in Nashville since they were usually accompanied by thrilling war newsreels. But no one could keep me from looking at the *Tennessean* where photographs of my own father leaving to train troops, soldiers in combat, sinking ships on fire, and black uniformed Nazis appeared frequently enough to enter my nightmares. TV was, of course, non-existent. I was allowed to listen to Bob Hope and Red Skeleton upstairs on my own bedside radio, and since there was only one radio downstairs, they couldn't keep me from hearing President Roosevelt's or Walter Winchell's broadcasts. For heroes most of us had fathers or uncles first. Second-tier heroes included Superman, Wonder Woman, and Captain Marvel, though I saw comic books almost as infrequently as I saw the Saturday afternoon serials. And nobody I knew threw a towel round their shoulders in hopes of imitating the male heroes' mantles, nor did girls girdle themselves in red, white and blue. Perhaps the airborne Superman and Marvel were too far above us. Rosie the Riveter, everybody said, was at work, but Wonder Woman was somebody else's dream. Tarzan was part of our lore, largely I suppose, because we'd seen him in a movie or a comic book and had grapevines to swing on in some of our yards. When we tired of quarrelling about who was going to be Tarzan, we tried smoking the vines...once. We didn't have a cap pistol among us. No one played cowboys and Indians. At school in the fifth grade our teacher taught us about a group of Northwest salmon fishing Indians. I knew nothing of other tribes, not even the Cherokee whose hunting grounds had been in Middle Tennessee.

While he was in the service, my father didn't write home often, but when he was assigned to Ft. Hood, Texas, he wrote one letter about studying rockets and going on rattlesnake hunts. I'd heard about V-2s but felt that, no matter how much he learned about them they were army secrets he'd never explain to me. And those poisonous snakes, I decided, were a particular kind he and other brave soldiers hunted and found curled up in caves. That was their business. I didn't think I'd venture into any Texas caves looking for them. By the time we crossed the Mississippi, I'd managed to dismiss the rattlesnakes. As far as real knowledge concerning Texas went, I probably had less going for me than one of those nineteenth century children trailing their parents in a covered wagon wandering westward.

Our parents knew we needed preparation for the move. They tried. My new mother told us about all her family. I already had relatives aplenty; I guessed a few more wouldn't hurt. We would have new aunts, uncles, cousins, but they were only a distant element in the uncertain future waiting out there. I was more curious about the part my father had already played; he'd taken two girls, daughters of Mother's friends just my age, on an afternoon fishing trip. I was immediately jealous; he often took my brother, but he'd never taken me fishing. He showed me a picture of these girls, standing arm in arm, both of them wearing shorts. Ann and Pat looked all right, but would I be welcome to link up with them? Mother, before she left home, had already talked to the teachers we would have. Most of them were friends of hers.

Before we left I'd overheard my aunts warning their brother about the narrowness of small town life; his only reply was it seemed to be a peaceful place and he needed some peace. In the excitement of the trip, I put aside the aunts' concerns. While traveling toward Texas, I remained mainly interested in Ann and Pat. They might have just been being polite to an older person; they might have just pretended to like going fishing. And even if their mothers knew my new mother, they might not want to know a girl with braces on her teeth and plain brown Arch-Preserver shoes on her feet either. I still didn't know what to do with my hair. Mostly it fell into limp straggles. My shoes were more worrisome. Nobody I knew in Tennessee, nobody I would know in Texas—

of this, I was certain—had to wear all-brown lace-up shoes. If Ann and Pat decided against them, they would decide against me. Much of the anxiety I had about the future was, I suspect, connected with those shoes.

I'd already had practice being the new kid—first in California when we followed my father out there in 1942. Being new didn't matter so much when you were seven and eight. Half a schoolroom could be new near an army post during the war. But being the new kid at Peabody, one of Nashville's well-established private schools, required a whole new set of adaptations. Not until the sixth grade had I begun to feel accepted. Now I had to leave hard-won friends to start all over.

Another larger problem waited: I was going to be skipped a grade. Pat and Ann and everyone else my age had already skipped the second grade when the twelve-year school system had been introduced in Texas. Since the schools I knew in Tennessee all had twelve grades, I thought the state of Texas must be sadly laggard. My father had told me when Mother was younger she'd ridden miles on horseback from her home in Evant, an even smaller town near Gatesville, to teach in a one-room country school. Because I admired her for riding so far to teach kids of all ages, I kept quiet about her state's backwardness. So involved in watching to see what happened next, I kept quiet often. This was not a trip merely to another army post, or to visit relatives we already knew; we were going to stay, and no matter what happened we would live in a little town in Texas.

Could I really manage to skip an entire grade? I'd just recently quit playing with my dollhouse. I was a reader, a daydreamer, a worrier. I knew how to swim, to play tennis though not well, to ride horseback English style in one of Nashville's parks, and in ballroom dancing classes, had learned to foxtrot and to waltz. I'd been introduced to horse shows, to operettas, to ballets, concerts, and country clubs. In school I did well in English, history, and geography, but was constitutionally weak in math and needed help with punctuation and spelling. Would I be equal to this giant leap over the seventh grade?

I worried all the way through Arkansas where my brother and I resumed our personal rivalry as if we'd never been apart. Since he'd been going to a public school where he hadn't been much of a student, he couldn't be skipped a grade. By the time we got to Texarkana, I'd often moved up to the front seat next to Mother while he ruled the back seat alone for many miles.

To reach Gatesville meant another day's drive, and when we arrived in early September I was surprised that it was still hot. September began fall in Tennessee. Here summer prevailed. East Texas had been fairly familiar looking, a lot like the part of Arkansas we'd driven through—pine woods and fields to wander over, creeks and rivers to cross; in the country everyone seemed to live in small white one story houses—many of them needing paint. In towns I saw some two-story houses, most of them looking as old as I was used to houses looking, probably built before the war plus leftover

Victorians, the kind of houses I'd known forever. As we traveled southwest, the country stretched toward plains; there were still low hills, but the landscape had a faded, tired look. Trees kept getting smaller. The night we drove into Gatesville it was too dark, and I was too tired to notice much. I could see we were going to live in one of those small white frame houses, one my father had rented on the corner of Pleasant Street, a name that sounded like something I'd read in a children's book. I went to bed, a strange one of Mother's, feeling like one of the *Five Little Peppers*. Fortunately my childhood reading included the *Peppers* and plenty of other books where families made their way through hard times by hard work and good spirits. Though I missed my aunts and grandmother, and the large gray brick house in Nashville, two parents and a brother, even if he was a tease, reclaimed me, and Texas was a new place. I think I began to believe in the fundamental superiority of the new, including people, books, clothes, and places all in one large lump.

This enthusiasm gave way soon to another reality; we were poorer than we'd ever been. (Much later I learned my father had given half of his army earnings to pay for our natural mother's hospitalization.) My ritual trips to the orthodontist would have to wait, not that I minded. During the first year in Texas, I would wear some of Mother's skirts cut down, but I didn't mind that either. My parents' after-the-war optimism as well as their newly wed determination to begin again directed our lives.

On a Monday, a few days after we got to Texas, Mother took Billy and me to school. I prevailed on her to let me wear my good pair of brown and white saddle Oxfords instead of the hated plain brown ones. I had a new navy dress with a sash to wear. After brushing my long hair, I stuck a barrette in one side to keep it out of my face. One of Mother's friends, a tall dark-haired lady greeted me with a kindly smile at the door to her eighth grade math class. I waited. Mother, half-hidden at my back, disappeared. I smiled when I was introduced to the class as if braces were normal and I was perfectly pleased to be there, and they could stare all day if they wanted. From previous introductions, I knew they would anyway. Then I went to the desk the teacher pointed out to me. At least it was the familiar worn brown wooden seat joined to a top with a hole for an ink bottle, the kind of desk I'd been sitting in since the first grade. I slid into it gratefully. My heart fell to my white shoelaces when I looked at the dense jumble of numbers chalked on the board. Then the girl in front of me who had a head full of brown curls turned around and whispered hello. It was Ann.

Pat was at another desk not far away. She and Ann stayed nearby all day. I met Cynthia and Chloris Ann in the next class and the two Sandras as well. Jean and Margaret Ann were a year ahead of us but part of the same group. All their mothers knew mine.

For the past three years I had been a student at a private school adjacent to Peabody Teacher's College. Architecturally based on Jefferson's design for the

University of Virginia, the college's main building—red brick with marble colonnades between—faced a vast green lawn nearly as large as an army parade ground. Peabody Demonstration School, across the street, reflected the college's bricks and columns. For recess we gathered on a well-mowed grassy field in the back.

A wide two-story red brick building, Gatesville High School, built on one of the few hills in town, had an arched entrance and curving front steps. No other ornamentation marked it. Widely rumored to be condemned, I didn't know who condemned it or why. The high school looked solid enough to me, and if I made it through the fearful eighth grade, I'd be there four more years. Around back of the high school building stood the old one-story, plastered-white-streaked-with-dust Junior High I attended. A weathered wooden army surplus barrack called The Band Hall took up the west side. The large separate white-streaked-with-dust plastered gym sat next to the high school. To the east, two tennis courts covered most of the ground. Protruding from the back of the high school's second floor was an enormous round metal covered slide, the fire escape. All buildings, except for the high school with its green patch in front, stood amidst dirt daily beaten to dust by student feet.

The first day I doubt that I consciously made comparisons between the luxurious grounds of my former school and the drabness of the present one. The differences were so extreme, I had too many other contrasts to get used to, and I must have been dazed by novelty.

I held my tongue and followed Ann and Pat to the cafeteria dug out a story beneath us in the back hillside of the Junior High.

There I was introduced to Texas institutional country cooking including such specialties as pinto beans cooked to a brown mush, slices of raw white onions, taco pie, and as a once a week treat, peach or apple cobbler made from canned peaches or apples. Some of my new friends brought their lunches. The rest of us bought ours and bolted them down. Pinto beans were so ever present on the menu in the days ahead I began to fantasize that tanker trucks were filled with the regulation mushy pintos then dispensed to schools throughout the state. Complaining about school food was universally acceptable; I might have easily complained with the rest of them, but didn't the first day. When up for approval, silence was safest. Immediately after lunch we escaped outside where the girls gathered to talk near the fire escape and a faucet jutting from the ground. I thought it an odd place to stand around, but there was no place to sit except the high school's front steps, naturally forbidden to younger students. Staring down I finally noticed my new friends in Gatesville Junior High did not wear brown and white saddle Oxfords. I eyed everyone else's loafers and wondered if I might be allowed to get a pair soon.

Whatever they may have thought, the girls I met at school were consistently welcoming. I'd never had so easy a first day. My father taking Ann and Pat fishing— they said it was fun—may have helped, but Mother actually was the one who made my introduction easier;

being her new daughter created quick acceptance. She'd lived in Gatesville most of her adult life, had been in business there, was known and liked. People wished her well, wished her new family well. And they didn't pry about the past; no one, young or old, asked me about my natural mother.

In spite of all the apparent goodwill, there were still apparent distinctions. Sometimes girls circled around me commanding, "Say water. Say poker." Fortunately they considered a southern accent comic. I never quite lost mine. Later Mother warned me, "Ann's mother says the girls are calling you 'Little Miss Nashville.'" Half proud, half defensive, I realized I'd relaxed enough to make comparisons out loud. It could have been what I thought an innocent remark about girls playing soccer, not basketball, at my Nashville school, but whatever I'd said, I had to stop mentioning the obvious differences.

I'd already asked my father privately, "What's wrong with the trees? They look stunted."

Many trees in Nashville grew at least eighty feet tall.

"Honey, I wouldn't mention that to anyone around here. They're pretty proud of their live oaks."

"Well, why does everything look so dusty?"

"Same reason the trees are lower...less rain." He'd put on his old army khakis, now minus insignia, and was getting ready to drive off. Taking Billy with him, he was on his way down to the warehouse where he was beginning to oversee Mother's business, a Texaco wholesale dealership. She didn't seem to mind. Later I discovered by the time she was forty-four she'd already tried many ways of living. She'd married, lost a stillborn child, divorced, taken over her alcoholic ex-husband's business, and asked a niece to live with her. When the niece left to marry, a friend moved in. When the friend left town, she lived alone. Beside the business, she owned a horse and a ranch she'd been adding acreage to since the early 1940s. After marrying my father she did a lot more cooking, took care of two children, and became more active in her bridge club and church. Was she part of that postwar trend, one of the thousands of women who moved out of jobs to let homecoming warriors take their places? If so, it was definitely by choice. Mother ran the dealership at a time when gasoline was strictly rationed and most male help went to the war effort Now my father hired two men to drive gas-filled tanker trucks around to service stations and do all sorts of other work including helping me or Billy saddle Mother's horse. We led Blaze from the corral just across from the warehouse's loading dock where Sam or Tom or whoever was around lifted the heavy western saddle onto his back. Some days after school I rode my bicycle to the warehouse, got the horse saddled, and walked him off to one of the almost empty dirt roads where I could ride at a good canter.

I'd had some experience of small towns, Paso Robles and Atascadero in California, both near the coastline, although I'd known they were, for us, merely temporary places. Franklin, my maternal grandmother's home in Tennessee, was the small town I knew best. A Confederate soldier stood on a plinth on the square. It was even more famous as a Civil War battlefield than Nashville. Age practically oozed out of its moss lined red brick sidewalks. The past lingered in its streets. Most everybody I met there knew my grandparents. Although my grandfather Truett had died in 1937, people had memories generations long.

"Sog," they recalled his nickname, "used to trade mules, farmed out there at the Pointer place." Years later when I began teaching Faulkner's short stories, I found myself on familiar ground immediately. In Nashville more people were acquainted with even more generations of my father's family.

Gatesville was all new territory. A whiff of its recent past remained; some sidewalks rose to a horseback rider's stirrup height above the streets, and over the walks, on two sides of the square, wooden awnings shaded front windows and anyone on foot. Mother knew the names of the owners of every business including the three movie theaters, the jeweler's, two clothing stores, two drugstores, a dry goods store, dime store, two banks, an army surplus store, car dealerships, and more. I went to school with many of their sons and daughters. Cynthia, Ann, Jean, and Pat, in 1946, the first year we were in Gatesville, lived in the same neighborhood, and we knew everyone who lived around us, not just the people who lived next door. Familiarity couldn't replace a long past, but it was comforting. If you began to know the names of people, you began to know some of the people. Gradually the newness wore off.

The town itself, with a population between four and

five thousand then, got its name from one of a string of federal frontier forts, Fort Gates, no longer visible. It had been located "near the river somewhere," Mother said. I didn't care about trying to find it; I'd toured enough forts.

In the center of the square Gatesville's glory stood. A courthouse built in 1897-1898; it was a mighty pile of limestone, its windows and doors outlined in dark orange sandstone, and statues of Justice with scales and swords waiting over two entrances. One of the few old buildings in town, it had many domes with four clock faces showing on the top one, and in 1946 on the very top of the clocks' dome, hung a bell that could be heard for miles. I hadn't known Nashville's courthouse location; Gatesville's was the center of the town's life. After the first of many trips around that building, I discovered it was the way people in town marked all sorts of occasions. Parades went round, bored teenagers went round—they dragged Main and drove round the courthouse like tracking an exclamation point with a fat period at the end. Sometimes we drove around the courthouse when we were returning from a vacation, or passed a driver's license test, or did well on an exam. Others made it when they graduated, or were celebrating a football team's victory, or had nothing else to do on a Saturday night.

The other old public building, one displayed in a small municipal park, was a log jail erected in 1858, said to be the only log jail still standing in Texas, a sad bit of history to show off, I thought at first. Soon I found people in town generally ignored it. A reminder of earlier times, it remained relentlessly empty; apparently there was little anyone could think to do with a log jail except to acknowledge its presence with a sign. More attention was given to the Texas State Boys' Reformatory located a few miles to the north. In past years big jailbreaks forced boys to run and hide all over town. A boy we knew at school lost his father who settled in the driver's seat just before an escaped state prisoner rose from the floor of the car's back seat and killed him. Fear led to wariness and locked doors, a practice contrary to my little town experience. West and east of the square just as the town faded away, ran the small, usually muddy Leon River named for one of the early Spanish explorers.

We'd been in town a while before I realized I hadn't seen many black people. As in Nashville segregation kept the children out of school. Eunice, Mother's black maid, came to our house on Pleasant Street one day a week to clean, iron, and on holidays like Thanksgiving—if we were having a lot of company—to help Mother cook and serve dinner.

She lived in the black part of town called "The Hill" where the Leon bent and a lumpy hill sloped down to meet it. Roads were unpaved, houses, largely unpainted. There were other poor people in town, of course, but on "The Hill," lived the poorest of the poor. Eunice, I learned when we took her home after work, had no street address. In Nashville I'd been made to memorize 1108 18th Avenue South in case I ever got lost. All the black people who worked there, Annie, Hattie, and

Owen, lived at well-known addresses. How did Eunice get her mail?

My father said she probably didn't get much, and probably the postman knew where she lived if she did receive a letter.

I thought he probably made up something just to satisfy my curiosity.

Eunice lived in a shabby, comfortable-looking little place at a certain curve in the dirt road near the river. The house, blessed by deep shade provided by a live oak tree and vines dangling from roof to porch, was enchanted looking; I thought if ever I needed, Eunice's place would be a wonderful hideout. I didn't think to question why I'd want a hideout or whether Eunice would be happy to have me. I simply took her care for granted. Visiting a farm in Tennessee when I was ten, I'd played with the black cook's children and thought nothing of it, but that was an isolated incident. By the time I was twelve segregation so divided my world it didn't occur to me to either question the division or wonder when one might step over it. Gradually, as I grew older, I realized my blindness.

Both Billy and I took to Eunice immediately. Through her I would find out a little about her life on "The Hill." Mother, working in the kitchen with her, knew much more. Eunice would talk about herself and her family but she didn't gossip about any of Mother's friends, and she worked for a number of them.

"Don't do no good to bear tales," she'd say both to admonish and to advise.

Her discretion combined with her good humor and cooking skill made her central to our lives. You could go to Eunice with any woe. In the years to come, she knew about every tangle I had with my parents, every boyfriend that caused me the least unhappiness. Sometimes she gave advice; generally she just listened. But there was an exchange. We knew something of her sorrows too; the sister who died young leaving Eunice to raise her daughter, the faithless second husband, the smart son who worked in California and never visited.

Whenever we drove down Main, Mother waved at various friends. The men she acknowledged wore regular business suits though some had western boots on too; the women all wore dresses and high heels. There were two or three men in cowboy hats and boots standing out in front of a cafe.

"Drugstore cowboys," she said.

I hadn't heard her speak so disdainfully about anyone else.

"They hang around town picking their teeth."

I would have to learn to recognize the variations. These were like the ones I'd seen in those Saturday matinees—pretend cowboys. The real ones must have been out working on ranches.

Mother worked on her father's ranch as a girl growing up, ridden horseback alongside him. She showed me the red satin shirt with pearlized buttons she'd worn when she guided her horse through some fancy footwork in rodeo quadrilles. Had she been a cowgirl? It seemed a little silly to call her one. This and a host of other questions stayed in my mind to be answered eventually. One was about language. There was the Leon River's name, the names of some of the streets, and words like "sabe" or "taco" Mother sometimes used. My father said I should learn Spanish. Who was I going to speak it to? I was assured there were Mexicans around, but I didn't see any I could identify. Only a little could be learned by looking at a town. It was all so new—a raw, dusty place with a horizon broken by stunted trees, a scrawny river, small brick, stone, or little white clapboard houses, every sort of Protestant church—the Baptist was the largest—a place where the sun wouldn't quit shining and drugstore cowboys decorated the streets.

Outside of town lived small farmers and ranchers. I couldn't understand the faint tone of derision I heard when people said, "dirt farmer." A farmer had to have dirt. It was years before I realized the term must have been a holdover from the days when there was a definite division between farmers and ranchers. The ghost of trail-driving times before hated barbed wire appeared was still apparent though the feud was largely forgotten. Knowing none of this at the time, I was soon saying "dirt farmer" with a slight sneer like everyone else.

⋯◄►⋯

Invaded by its countrymen during the war, Gatesville soon emptied of soldiers from everywhere, and settled down with its own share of veterans, my father included. Residual bitterness remained in the country over losses of farms and small ranches devoured by the establishment of Ft. Hood. People didn't forget the sight of their homes' chimneys still standing, lone reminders of their territory, on what became part of an army reservation. Unable to buy other land, those farmers and ranchers either left the country to work in nearby towns or began their lives over in other ways during the war. They were the first among many to choose another direction.

All over Texas a majority of people slowly began to leave the country, to go to larger towns and cities, something I couldn't have possibly discerned in the forties, but realized later I'd lived when an older, far more rural past, was part of everyday life. Farmers and their families still came to town on Saturdays; most of the children went to little schools dotted round the countryside until the schools were consolidated in Gatesville in the fifties. Horses could be ridden safely any time on any street except Main. When your horse needed new shoes, you rode it three or four miles to the blacksmith's, a trip I made repeatedly with Ann McClellan whose family also kept a horse corralled in town. If we especially wanted fresh eggs, we bought them from somebody's small farm on the outskirts, and ice, when a large amount was needed, we bought from the icehouse, until air-conditioning arrived, the only place in town you could hope to shiver in the summer. After the courthouse bell tolled noon, men drove home to hot lunches.

Some changes were evident earlier. Two of Mother's sisters had married men from cities; they lived in Dallas and Galveston, but her two brothers, brought up as ranchers, remained ranchers. The youngest one lived west of Evant, the small place where Mother had been born and where her mother still lived thirty miles from Gatesville. Taken to meet Uncle Tommy, his wife, and sons at a family supper, Billy and I disgraced ourselves by complaining the enchiladas were too hot to eat. Pepper, except for a sprinkling of a few black specks and the tiniest bit of cayenne occasionally, had not been part of our bland diets. My two new boy cousins laughed at my brother and me when we drank all our water and asked for more. I showed even worse ignorance by posting English style while riding on one of their quarter horses.

"What you jumping up in the saddle for?" The oldest one demanded.

"This horse has the rockiest trot I ever rode. If I rise a little—"

"You're supposed to sit down in the saddle."

I kept posting.

Those boys wore boots and cowboy hats every day. They had practically grown up sitting in their western saddles. Furthermore they had a terrible prejudice against English saddles, which they called "useless postage stamps." I argued every jockey and jumper rode them. If they had ever seen anything like the Iroquois Steeple Chase held every May in Nashville, they wouldn't have jeered so easily.

"Little bitty old saddles are useless on a cattle ranch," they said.

"Bet you can't stay on one," I insisted just as a jackrabbit skittered out of the brush and my horse shied wildly around it.

The boys nearly fell off their own horses laughing at me clinging to the saddle horn. Nevertheless, like all of our new relatives, they treated us as if we'd been kin forever. We might not ride western style as well as they did, nor were we used to jalapeño-flavored dishes but we were acceptable.

Slowly we met the rest of the family, driving down to Uvalde, and on to the border town of Nuevo Laredo, where I heard Spanish spoken and recognized Mexicans for the first time in my life. My brother and I stuffed ourselves with cajeta we bought at the market while the grown-ups were busy bargaining about something else. When they discovered the cajeta, they said awful things about goats' milk and took it away from us as if we'd endangered our health. We licked the caramelized crumbs from the sides of our lips and became lifelong devotees of cajeta. The uncle in Uvalde was a rancher named Buck. He had a wife, a daughter, and a son called Buck, Junior. Texas names weren't really any stranger than those in Tennessee. I added the Uvalde group to my list. Altogether my brother and I had acquired a new grandmother, five new cousins and eight new aunts and uncles. We had to wait till Christmas to meet the ones from Dallas. Those living in Galveston, Billy and Bess McDonald, were childless. I was told that their house had been built by Uncle Billy's father, a Scottish sea captain, who, after landing, had dismantled his ship and used the timbers for his new foundation

We met them first in San Antonio, a halfway point between Gatesville and Galveston, and because the adults needed time alone, my brother and I were sent off on a sightseeing bus carrying us to the Spanish missions around the city ending at the Alamo. When I walked in I saw a sign saying over 200 Tennesseans had fought and died there in 1836. After four war years spent honoring soldiers, I was shocked into an immediate connection. I was in the middle of eighth-grade Texas history, something everyone else already knew and I had to learn. The rudiments of Tennessee history, especially Nashville's, had seeped down to me. Perhaps because I had to learn it all at once, Texas history, until then, seemed something people had stored up and brought out to prove their native pride. Since other states' histories were of little importance, I felt self-righteously huffy about the subject. But after seeing those numbers at the Alamo, I knew I was part of a common past.

We ate our first Christmas dinner, a meal stretched into the evening, at Uncle Tommy's ranch house. Though Uncle Buck and his family were missing, Granny Winters, as well as Mother's sister from Dallas, her husband, and daughter were there. Mother stayed to help clean up while our father drove us home in his new red pickup. Though he'd promised Mother to give up whiskey when they married, he'd been drinking with the rest of the men in the den behind the kitchen. Unfortunately he got drunk easily; two drinks and he was gone, transformed from the person we'd always relied on to a scary, mumbling stranger.

We hadn't been on the road long when he said, "I don't know what happened to Katherine."

Billy and I sat as still as we could in the seat beside him.

"Don't understand how...your mother—I don't know what happened."

He quieted and drove on muttering phrases we couldn't understand now and then in an undertone.

My brother and I stared silently out at the darkness, at the white line on the highway, which luckily we weren't weaving over. But I wavered inside all the rest of the way back, wondering what my father meant, why he felt as he did, and why our natural mother's illness was so bad he had to be drunk to talk about it. This was the only time she had been mentioned since we'd moved to Texas.

When we walked through the back yard of the house, Billy grabbed our big Irish setter out of his pen—he was always kept outside—and dragged the dog by the collar to bed with him in his room next door to our parents' room where our father was rambling back and forth.

Mother must not have spoken to him before checking on Billy.

"Why is Rusty in your bed?"

Billy wouldn't answer.

From the doorway to my room across the hall, I whispered, "He's scared."

"Bill!" She called to my father, went into their room, and shut the door.

I used to wonder what she said to him when she discovered he'd broken his promise.

—————

That Christmas morning Billy and I had been given our first pair of boots, which we wore all day long. On weekends we wore them out to Mother's ranch, land she owned but leased to Uncle Tommy for grazing cattle, where we found more new country to explore. In the summer Mother showed us Mexican plums to gather for jelly and in the fall our father pointed out native pecans for pies.

At the end of May the school year was over and we'd moved to another larger house; I passed to the ninth grade still constitutionally weak in math, still in need of repair in spelling and punctuation. But no one circled round me any more commanding, "Say water. Say poker." I had lost my novelty value; they got used to me. I'd learned their language. A sudden wind so harsh it turned the weather cold was "a norther." Any one too self-important was "a swole toad," or they had "the big head." In the grass the awful stickers that kept everybody from going barefoot were "grass burrs." A farmer of German descent was a "Dutchman." Low growing brush at the ranch was called "shinnery." A few years later when the widespread county schools were consolidated and all the new country kids came into Gatesville, I was one more town girl.

Slowly I'd discovered the small town had its charms. We could walk and ride all over it on our bicycles. On Blaze, Mother's well-gaited Morgan horse, Billy and I took turns riding; we were allowed to cover as much of the country as we wanted.

My brother apparently was born to explore; the urge came upon me later. The unknown territory around Gatesville held mysteries my friend Ann and I had to discover. On a previous ride we'd led our horses over the rickety plank bridge at Fauntleroy's Crossing on the way to Lone Mountain, a hill poking above somebody's pasture and not high enough, in my estimation, to deserve being called a mountain. We might have headed in another direction, but we chose instead one fall afternoon to ride east to Mound. Like some other small settlements nearby—the most obvious being Flat—it had acquired a geographical name, this one from a small chalk hill nearby. We thought we knew some boys at school who lived there; however, we didn't know its distance from town. Destination, to someplace we'd never been, beckoned. When we finally reached the settlement, we found an empty street, no boys or anyone else, a small collection of houses and a one-pump filling station where we stopped to get a soda. Inside I borrowed the grumpy manager's phone to call Mother. Rather proudly I announced we had arrived in Mound.

"You've ridden too far," she said. "That's eight miles away. Get back on that horse and get home before sundown."

Mother seldom sounded so alarmed and angry, so I knew we'd have to ride hard to make her deadline. Already my inner thighs were chaffed from the ride out in green woolen pants. We loped toward home as long as I could stand the chaffing, then I'd have to stop and ride sideways by throwing one leg over the saddle horn until I thought I could bear a lope again. Ann kindly kept pace with me even though she was sure her mother would be as mad as mine if we returned late. We both kept our eyes on the dipping sun watching it slip down faster and faster. Clouds gathered round it. By afterglow we reached home in time to understand the wretched truism: "As far as you ride out, you have to ride back."

When it grew too hot to ride horseback, there was a public swimming pool in the City Park where I spent most of the summer afternoons before air conditioning, and in July a rodeo appeared.

The first afternoon before the rodeo began, despite the heat, all my friends and I rode in the parade on horseback or floats consisting mainly of trucks with signs and trailing crepe paper. So many of us rode on the city pool's float in the parade I questioned who was going to watch it. Having to smile the whole way, wearing our bathing suits, moving slowly the length of Main Street in July—I had draped myself over one of the truck's front tire fenders—wasn't as glamorous as we'd first thought.

"When you've seen one rodeo, you've seen them all," Mother said when she refused to accompany us to our first one. Billy and I went with our friends. In succeeding summers, I agreed with Mother. At the first one I couldn't like the way horses and bulls were roweled, or the way the clown ran out in the middle of the arena and faked fear, then had to hide in a barrel when in real danger. In time, I realized rodeos had a ritual aspect; perhaps to some people it was a reenactment of a treasured past, but it was never mine.

Just before a seven year drought dried up everything, we picnicked and swam in some of the larger surrounding creeks, favorite excursions at fifteen and sixteen, when we got old enough to drive and were still young enough to have to hide our cigarettes. In those same high school years, I caught a variety of the football fever that rages through the state and was elected cheerleader for two years. By my senior year, I became the editor of "Dirt," the title of a page in the high school newspaper. In this job I was allowed to write a two-column page of hearsay published in purple ditto machine print, about what everyone was doing and especially who was dating whom. But I would always stand a little apart. Like any immigrant, I carried my own past with me and for many summers, still without seeing my first mother, I went back to Nashville for weeks at a time, though I always returned to Texas. Finally, along with other graduates who were sure they had outgrown the town, after living five years in Gatesville, I left to go to college at the University of Texas in Austin. I married a Texan, had our children here, buried my dead, those in my immediate family, here.

However it was during 1946 and 1947, our first period in Texas after the war, I realized we'd reached a new home. My brother, in the habit of running away from school, quit running since there was always someone who knew where you were, both a disadvantage and an advantage. Small town nosiness led to gossip just as it did in cities; the only difference was it took less time to circulate. While we were young, living there was a form of protection. Being known by almost everyone, we began to know almost everyone. Rather than narrowing our experience by living in a small town, our world expanded.

IV.

Returning to Tennessee

I went back to Nashville almost every summer while in high school and during some summers afterward. The first two times I rode the Cotton Belt, boarding one of the Pullman cars in Waco, thirty-eight miles from Gatesville. After sleeping through most of Arkansas, I changed to the L&N in Memphis. Coming to Nashville and going back to Texas, my aunts arranged for distant cousins who lived in Memphis to show up at the station and make sure I changed trains safely. I knew I could do this on my own, however they insisted on continuing to look after me.

On its usual schedule, the L&N arrived to deliver passengers shortly after noon to a vast noisy shed behind Nashville's Union Station. Aunt Elnora and Aunt Dorothy would be waiting at the platform to meet me. We climbed a metal stairway to walk through the immense main waiting room where light filtered down through amber colored stained glass and our footsteps echoed on the tile floor. Immediately afterward we drove to lunch at the Hermitage Hotel, named after Andrew Jackson's home, a scheme, like others my aunts had, to encourage me to remember my roots, like Jackson's, were in Tennessee.

Whether I spent three weeks or four, time was divided exactly between my parents' families, the way perhaps any child of divorced parents would recognize, but I didn't. I hadn't considered the many results of a legal division. I simply thought I had two mothers, one in Texas, the other in a Tennessee hospital, and failed to notice how carefully the Truetts and the Culberts measured my days until I suggested I'd like to spend more time with one or the other and learned I couldn't because, my aunts explained, "it wouldn't be fair." Each visit had to be divided three ways; a number of days at 1108 with Aunt Elnora, then Aunt Dorothy and Uncle Fred's house, then an equal number of days in Franklin with Grandmother Truett where I'd see Mother's brother, Uncle Felix. From there I'd make short trips back to visit my Mother's sister, Thelma, and her husband, Nelson, who'd moved to Nashville from Franklin. None of them mentioned Mother.

I must have thought I wasn't supposed to question anyone about her but I did, and the first ones I asked were, to my mind, the ones easiest to approach, Aunt Thelma and Uncle Nelson. Aunt Thelma was gentle, though nervous and fluttery—early signs of her own unnamed mental problems. "Sweet" was her designation in the family, which meant, though usually a quiet person, she was a great comforter, especially to children, as well as her mother and husband. Her son called her "Dear." Uncle Nelson represented the practical side of life; he worked for an insurance company, employment that suited him precisely. A caring man, his self-selected position in the family and out of it, was to look after needy elderly people.

To me he was always kind. When I asked about Mother, he let me know he and Aunt Thelma had visited her, and she was all right, an invariable reply for many summers.

Now I question my silent reaction to this pronouncement. Why couldn't I have asked exactly what he meant? Didn't I wonder if she remembered my brother and me? Perhaps I thought she'd forgotten us and I feared to ask if she had. Perhaps I'd transferred all emotional reliance to my stepmother. I don't think this was so, for I never forgot Katherine Truett was my mother though she'd grown increasingly distant as the city I'd known and my childhood friends had.

The medical rule in the forties of separating children from mental patients lasted through the fifties, or perhaps the adults in my life thought the rule extended

*Katherine Truett Culbert and her children: Carolyn, six,
and Billy, four, 1940, in the front yard, Nashville.*

that far, or maybe because they were so accustomed to keeping us parted and still so threatened by what they felt was the shame of mental illness in the family, they didn't know what to do later.

Before my father, my new mother, my brother and I left for Texas, Aunt Thelma had given me an eight-by-ten picture of Mother sitting on a low rock wall dividing the front yard of our house from the woods nearby. Light fell through the trees on a pretty, dark-eyed, dark-haired woman looking quite self possessed with her two children, Billy, sitting on the wall beside her, me standing. She must have planned to have the photograph made, for she had on a white blouse with a softly ruffled collar, a dark skirt, and high heels. Billy and I were in our Sunday best. It was taken before the war when she was approximately thirty-three and Billy and I were four and six. There are other pictures Aunt Thelma and Uncle Nelson gave me later, including a classic sepia-toned late Victorian looking one of Grandmother Truett with her children. Here Mother's wearing a large bow on top of her head and clinging to her brother's arm. There's a snapshot taken sometime in her teens of her in an English riding habit, her derby hat cocked to one side. In her mouth she holds as horse show winners held—their hands being full of reins—a prize medallion streaming with ribbons. She's not on horseback but is standing on the sidewalk in front of the porch of Grandmother's house.

In another, posed in front of a Peabody College building after her graduation with a Bachelor of Science degree in 1928, she wore her cap and gown. Then there are a series made by a professional. In these she's become a beauty, smiling serenely, wearing in one, a cloche, that helmet-like, close-fitting hat women wore in the 1920s. These were evidently studio portraits, part of a portfolio, made after she graduated and had a short fling at modeling, for they were followed by a newspaper picture of her on a poster in aviator's gear. Another studio picture shows her in her wedding dress, long veil falling behind her head, a gauzy train hemmed with lace spread around her on the floor.

Chronologically the picture of the three of us sitting on a couch along with Aunt Dorothy and Uncle Fred, dressed in his Army Air Corps uniform, comes last. Billy is making a face at the photographer. Uncle Fred looks amused, Aunt Dorothy is vaguely worried, and Mother looks absolutely haggard. Looking at all of the photos, no one would think she was the same person as the proud young mother with her two children.

Someone destroyed all of the other photographs of her in the one album I saw. I never knew who but suspected my grandmother Truett, in her bitterness about the divorce, had torn out all the snapshots including Mother and my father.

When I moved to Texas, the picture of the three of us at the wall with the forest behind us was the only one I owned. I hid it in the bottom of a drawer under my clothes. From time to time, especially when feeling sad, I would slip it out and stare at it briefly. I was aware it was an idealized version of us all; nevertheless, the picture was my talisman, a part of a past life. Though I offered, my bother refused to look at it.

In the future as I grew older, during my senior year in high school and after I'd begun college, I went back to Nashville by plane, and every time we landed at the airport across the road from Central State Mental Hospital where my lost mother still lived. This proximity, just the faint sight of the buildings, worried me so much I began to ask Aunt Dorothy, the aunt I felt closest to, questions. Somehow I was sure, except for my father, she knew more than anyone else. And I started at a safe distance, back in 1943.

"Why do you think Mother wanted to go to Pennsylvania?"

"I don't know. She thought your aunt Allie was someone who could understand her problems I guess. When I saw you and Billy get on that train with her, Katherine turned to me and said, 'Dorothy, if anything happens to me, look after my children.'"

"You must have said you would."

"I was worrying about Fred already gone to India and Brother in California, who was supposed to go overseas at any time. All I told her was, 'Katherine, nothing's going to happen to you.'"

"It was the sort of thing one said to an uneasy sister-in-law getting on a train. In wartime real worry was spent on men, on your own, on everyone's. We should have worried more about Katherine. Nobody knew much about mental illness then, about symptoms. I knew about the Menninger Clinic in Kansas, but I wasn't the one in charge of her treatment. Your grandmother and Felix, and your father were."

Little by little I began to get more answers. Sometime in my twenties when I was visiting her, Aunt Dorothy, again, was the one who revealed Mother had tried to hang herself in the basement of the yellow brick house in Kittanning. Aunt Allie, the aunt we were staying with, admitted that Mother had previously begun to wear a bathing suit under her dress, so suicidal ideas—the Allegheny being close—must have been occurring for some time. Uncle Gerald and Aunt Allie cut her down from a basement pipe and called the hospital while we were still away at the birthday party.

"We all worried for a while that the blood flow to the brain had been stopped long enough to damage it, but the doctors said it hadn't."

Sitting on the sofa in her living room beside Aunt Dorothy, I remained in wordless shock, staring at the red and blue Oriental rug in front of the fireplace. Its whirling designs looked as intricate as my mother's motivations seemed to have been. How had she come to that? Why would she try to take her life? Suspended in total bewilderment, I had to find out everything later in infuriating bits.

My grandmother Truett, a great admirer of spas as she went to them to treat her arthritis and to escape from ragweed pollen, decided to take Mother from the Pennsylvania hospital to one or more of them. Doctors might have advised her to do so. A series of warm and cold baths was one of the regimens suggested then for nervous problems. Finally before being transferred to Central State in Nashville, Mother was sent to an osteopathic sanatorium in Missouri, though why this place was chosen, I don't know. Her doctor's letters are my only written medical records about her health.

January 18, 1944

She has been quite disturbed and upset, particularly in regard to her children. Sometimes she will say that she has enough. Then, the next day, she will make the statement that she would have several more....

...the nurses report that she begins talking about various things, indicating delusions of reference and that her orientation as regards time and place are somewhat disturbed."

January 25, 1944

...lately she has again become increasingly agitated and upset over various ideas which she is trying to straighten out in her mind...I have found that she has become more confused as to where she is, and she is laboring under quite a few delusional ideas...the outlook cannot be considered too favorable.

February 1, 1944

...She feels that her trouble is all caused by the fact that her home life has been disrupted by the war, and it is possible that this has contributed somewhat...although it would not be considered entirely to blame....

...She asks me occasionally about her children and as to how many she has and whether they are being properly cared for. I always try to reassure her...and it seems to help for a short while.

...the patient might make a recovery, particularly as long as she does not become completely dissociated from reality.

June 7, 1944

...Her conversation is becoming gradually more incoherent and difficult to follow, which indicates increasing detachment from reality. If you should care to have the patient receive the electric shock treatment or insulin shock, if you will let me know, we can make the necessary preparations for it.

I don't know if she was given the proposed shock treatments. Until after my father, both of his sisters, and my grandmother Truett died, these letters were kept from me. Aunt Dorothy had hidden them in a black tin box my Grandfather Culbert stored his business receipts in. This was in turn stored in another relative's basement with instructions to give it to me after Aunt Dorothy's death. Merely seeing it, I thought, "secrets." Opening the box, reading the doctor's letters, I realized once more, especially since Mother was confused about the number of her children, the whole family's desire to protect me and my brother.

In the meantime, I did more research.

I went to see one of her close friends in Nashville, Kay White. There were others, but she was the one I remembered best probably because she had a daughter my age Mother used to take me to play with. I asked Kay what she'd known about Mother's state of mind after we came back to Tennessee from California in 1943.

"That time before she left for Pennsylvania, she was often exhausted from lack of sleep. When she came to see me, I talked her into lying on the bed and listening to music some afternoons. I tried to get her to at least take a nap. But no matter what I tried, I couldn't get her to calm down enough to rest."

The pediatrician who'd looked after my brother and me lived next door to Aunt Dorothy, so I questioned him too. He was a short, cherubic looking man who laughed easily, a person I'd liked as a child.

With some remorse, he said, "She came to me and said, 'I think I'm losing my mind.'"

"Nonsense, Katherine!" he told her. "Those who think they're going crazy never do."

Obviously he was the wrong kind of doctor and just as obviously, he only repeated what most people, even well-meaning ones, said at the time. For a long time I remained angry at his blindness and his willingness to rely on a commonplace saying.

Early in 1967, I was thirty-three, married with three children, when I finally totally reacted against my family's protective silence, prompted in part by my own problems with manic-depression and the psychiatrist who was treating me for it.

"Do you think," he asked, "it's better to know about your mother or not to know?"

I was educated. I had two degrees, a B.J. and an M.A., and I realized I'd been stumbling around in utter ignorance. In fact I'd been keeping myself from knowing; I was as willfully blind as our pediatrician had been.

"I'd better know," I said at my next session.

My doctor gave me articles to read about schizophrenia. I learned of the various studies made on the disease and the difficulty of treating it. I also found schizophrenia isn't an illness that splits personality in two parts—there's no Jekyll and Hyde division; instead the mind seemed to be divided into fragments. The psychiatrist assured me that even institutionalized schizophrenics had lives of their own, not like ours certainly, but it was thought that they lived in the kind of world we live in during our dreams, entering and leaving places whose reality we don't question, nor do we question how we got there. Patients knew their surroundings at times, had friends, had feelings, though they were often emotionally withdrawn.

My brother refused to talk about her or to consider going with me to see our Mother.

"She's nothing but a vegetable," he said.

"She's not!" I countered then realized we were arguing like children once more. I had to give up the fight when I understood he'd given all his loyalty to our stepmother; possibly he also felt more comfortable or safer remaining within well-known territory.

I could understand. After all, I'd lived in the same territory.

My father continued all his life to contribute to her hospital bill, and checked on her when he returned to Tennessee for his mother's funeral, as well as when he took our second mother to Nashville to visit his sisters. Though he could be quick tempered, he was a man of few words in an emotional crisis. To his sisters in November of 1943, after reporting his wife showed no improvement, he wrote from his post in California, "This letter seems so matter of fact, but I'm so broken up over this I don't know any other way to tell you all the story." Although Mother called their family lawyer by name—he sometimes accompanied my father on his visits to the hospital—she never recognized her ex-husband. He suffered unreasonably for this since he partially blamed himself for her illness.

Reading those letters from the doctor in Missouri I have now, it is possible to see that, in hindsight, she probably had some form of schizophrenia, but the doctor at the sanatorium found it impossible to give it a name. The first DSM—the *Diagnostic and Statistical Manual of Mental Disorders*—which describes and classifies mental disorders was not been published until 1952, nine years after Mother was hospitalized. The first medication, Thorazine, used for schizophrenia, hadn't been discovered until sometime during the war and wasn't used in this country until 1954. Even now the complex causes of schizophrenia remain unknown. If genetics are involved, the answer hasn't yet been unraveled.

By the sixties, when I'd determined I had to see Mother, medical fashion had changed entirely. Everyone in a mental patient's family is now invited, indeed encouraged, to visit.

"Your mother's ill. She's in the hospital. We're going to see her." That's what doctors tell fathers to say now. "Hospitals exist for all sorts of sick people; we have mental hospitals for the mentally ill."

⋯—◆—⋯

I went to Tennessee's Central State Mental Hospital with Uncle Nelson, one of the few people she had always recognized, and my husband. The three of us sat on the front porch of one of the red brick buildings, waiting to go in, and while we sat there, a squirrel scrabbled up on the porch and began cracking a nut. I watched it wanting to laugh and cry at the same time. There we were, at the nuthouse, a place I'd known about and, without realizing it, had feared for years.

Called inside to meet Mother's doctor, by his accent a European immigrant, though I couldn't place his native country. He gave me permission to see her, but cautioned, "You cannot cry. It will upset her too much."

A nurse led the three of us to a ward on a third story where there were plenty of windows and the beds were all lined up. Though uniform in size, they didn't look like hospital beds since each one had a different kind of quilt or spread on it. All the women, every one about my mother's age, wore ordinary clothes, printed cotton housedresses they would have worn in the forties, the kind of dresses older women still wore around the house. The nurse led us down an L-shaped aisle and around its corner aisle to my mother, a thin gray-haired, fifty-six-year-old woman I had never seen before. I wouldn't have known who she was if I'd seen her on the street; nor did she recognize me. I had no intimate feelings for her, no sudden swell of emotion, no withheld tears. It was as if I were the withdrawn one.

"Who are you?" The nurse, by the tone of her voice, seemed to be asking her a rote question.

"Katherine Culbert...Katherine Truett Culbert." Her monotone answer was just as rote, but as we walked out of the ward with her, various women sitting on their beds or standing in the aisle all along the way to the door said, "Hello, Katherine." "How are you, Katherine?"

Were these the friends, I wondered? She nodded to them though she didn't speak. Sometimes she made a little waving motion with one hand.

We entered an elevator to go downstairs, and as I looked around I saw I couldn't tell the patients from the visitors. Everybody appeared as ordinary as we did. No one was throwing their arms around, or crying aloud, or threatening anyone; we were only a group of people going to the ground floor. Away from the building, the four of us sat on a bench surrounded by green, park-like grounds. They were mowed, not planted with flowers or bushes, and meandered pleasantly through trees all around the buildings.

Sitting next to her, I told Mother exactly what her doctor had said I should.

"I'm your daughter, Carolyn. I was a little girl the last time you saw me. Now I'm grown up and I've come to see you. Billy couldn't come, so I brought his picture."

I gave her a small black and white snapshot of my brother. She glanced at it and immediately tucked the picture in her brassiere. The doctor later said it was a maternal gesture and I thought, since Billy was her youngest, the one she'd worried about most, he was probably right.

Uncle Nelson handed Mother the orange juice we'd bought for her. Because she especially liked it, he carried some every time he went to visit her. She drank it as a child is liable to accept a treat, all at once, too fast Uncle Nelson thought, as he kept warning her to slow down and not to spill. We tried to make a kind of conversation about the weather, the color of the day, how gray it was. Mother would mumble a bit only when asked a direct question and most times she'd only nod or shake her head. Her name, when asked by the nurse, was the only thing she said that I could truly understand. We took her to the elevator, returned with her to her ward, and I went back to see her doctor to report, except for her taking the picture, the lack of much reaction. I had to ask what I already felt was a hopeless question.

"The new drugs…can't any of them help her?" I knew by then that I'd been helped by antidepressants.

He shook his head. "If you tied your arm to your side for years, you wouldn't be able to use it. That's what has happened to her brain. We have found certain pathways in the schizophrenic brain are used over and over. The rest atrophy. The drugs can sometimes help others, other younger patients."

She was born too early.

"I have been talking to some of the family and to one of her friends. They say she didn't have much self-confidence."

"Schizophrenia can happen to anybody, the ultra-confident, the unconfident, men, women, intelligent, unintelligent, educated, uneducated, anyone." He swept his arm over his desk as if to account for all possibilities.

I asked what could be done for her, what I could do. He shrugged gently and suggested I send her postcards now and then but not to expect an answer. I didn't cry until I was in the car once more, and I cried then for the shell of a person she'd become, as well as for the loss of the mother I'd known.

Following that first visit to the hospital, my husband and I stayed on in Nashville for a while with Aunt Dorothy.

"You must feel like a wind has blown through your head clearing away all the cobwebs," she said and I agreed.

In Texas once more my father and second mother made a special trip to Salado, a little town halfway between Gatesville and Austin, to meet my husband and me. It was a Sunday just after we'd returned from Nashville. We met in the small side garden of a restaurant we all liked.

After greeting us, the first thing my father said was, "I'm glad you saw her." Then he patted me on the back. "She didn't...?

"How could she know me? I couldn't recognize her."

He nodded, and I knew he was relieved.

As for my brother, no amount of insisting it was better to know than to imagine would change his mind.

He would listen to whatever I told him about our mother, but it became clear he preferred to know second-hand.

I later learned that Grandmother Truett, the only one in the family who would not give up hope, had taken Mother to her home in Franklin, thinking she might be able to live with her, but Mother begged to return to Central State. The institution had become her home. Why, I wondered, hadn't my grandmother ever told me she made this attempt? Even if I lived in Texas, I could have come to see Mother then. Perhaps Grandmother needed to prove she could take care of her daughter first; perhaps she feared Mother's reactions. And I think, of course, sparing the children had become etched in her mind. There is no way to know all of someone else's reasons.

Soon after Grandmother died, Uncle Felix, her only son, who had been appointed my mother's guardian, suffered such poor health that he asked me to become her guardian. Legally this amounted to little more than looking after the money left to her by Grandmother, reporting my book-keeping to the state of Tennessee, and making decisions about her welfare. It wasn't a hard task; sadly, most of those decisions had already been made.

There were other visits to the hospital, and in each one, as Mother aged, she was worse, and her surroundings were worse. When I went to visit after she was convalescing from surgery for a duodenal ulcer, the acrid odor of urine and disinfectant in the ward for the bedridden at the mental hospital smelled almost unbearable. The doctors I checked with told me they never got used to it. In 1973, the last time my husband and I saw her, a pitiable crowd of old, quite mad women in housedresses almost surrounded us when we first walked in. Probably they were some of the ambulatory schizophrenic women I'd seen in the other ward years before; these were Mother's group of women, all born too early. I smoked then, and they must have smelled it on me, but they didn't have the words to ask for a cigarette, only gestures, two fingers held together patting their lips. The attendant in charge shook her head when I tried to give Mother my pack. As the one person on duty, she couldn't oversee all those women smoking. My offer was as futile as writing the postcards had been.

The attendant advised me to tell her of my brother's death in an accident. After many disastrous starts, he had finally found what he wanted to do with his life and became a successful rancher. When he was thirty-six, seven months before he died, he married a woman with four children. Driving his pick-up home one night, he somehow lost control, swerved off the road to a drainage ditch, and rammed into the open end of a metal culvert. The force of the collision pushed him through the windshield and killed him instantly. We were still asking questions about what made him swerve, questions we knew could never be completely answered. He died on the last day of March. My husband and I came back to Tennessee to see Mother in April. Our grief over this loss was still raw. Remembering the doctor's warning years before against upsetting her, I waited, uncertain whether to tell her or not. But finally when I did, she had absolutely no reaction to the news of Billy's death. By then I understood her withdrawal was complete. For a moment I even envied her this lack of feeling but only for a moment.

One morning someone from the hospital's administration called me in Texas to tell me she had become senile. The news she was senile as well as schizophrenic was so strange; I didn't know such a combination was possible.

The woman added that if I would settle Mother's bill, they could send her to a nursing home, which would be the best place for her. In this way, the new Medicaid laws could help empty mental hospitals. During his lifetime my father had always paid the hospital part of the bill per month, and my brother and I were prepared to take over that charge. To allow her to go to the nursing home, I followed a Tennessee lawyer's advice and paid the hospital the inheritance she'd received from Grandmother Truett. In Mother's name, I was allowed to keep fifteen hundred dollars, the amount enough for anyone's burial, the government had ruled. She was then legally impoverished.

Uncle Nelson continued to be the one member of the family to see Mother. Aunt Thelma had mental problems of her own; her hold on normality was too tenuous to allow her further grief. Grandmother Truett had died in 1968, as had my father. Uncle Felix, felt as unable as Aunt Thelma to visit his sister. In the years Mother remained institutionalized, he'd seen her only once when she went to an ordinary hospital for the ulcer surgery. My husband and I were still in Texas, raising children, working, living our lives. My visits were infrequent, and I finally acknowledged how painful it was for me to make the trip. At first I felt terribly guilty, for I had wanted so much to see her again, to help her if I could. Later I confessed to Uncle Nelson and Aunt Thelma I had reached the point—as the doctors had said so many years before—where my presence helped neither of us. I'd half expected them to be angry. Instead they were accepting.

"We understand. It's hard to see Katherine," said Uncle Nelson, whose benevolence I'd relied on for years. He called early in 1978 to say Mother had died; evidently she had a heart attack when she fell out of a chair. She was 71.

We buried Mother after a private graveside ceremony on a sunny January afternoon in the family plot in Franklin, Tennessee. All I could think was, "She's free now."

Noises On

Five of us in a line in the middle of the gym had just finished leading a cheer when laughter rose around us.

One of the other girls in line pointed to the floor, "Your skirt!"

What could be wrong with my skirt? It was the same kind of cotton print with a ruffle on the bottom and trimmed with lace that everyone wore that spring.

Turning slowly, I found a torn white eyelet dripping down to the varnished gym floor and outlining my heels. The principal, leaning against the wall at the south end of the gym, his arms crossed on his chest, overseeing the contest as he oversaw everything, beckoned me toward him.

I shook my head. Why did he think I should quit? Contest rules demanded we lead two yells. By the time I'd finished the second one, laughter rising high again, and the standing voters multiplying when the football players stood up in unison, told me I was one of Gatesville High's new cheerleaders. Friends who were majorettes had suggested trying out. Football fever pervaded our school lives; I succumbed easily. Transplanted to Texas, I knew almost nothing about football. It hadn't been played in my grammar school. During the war the men in my family, except for one 4-F uncle, were gone soldiering. In our household full of womenfolk, football was never mentioned. By skipping a grade after moving to Texas, I'd been catapulted from elementary into junior high school in unknown country where people were football crazy.

The afternoon after the contest I walked home half-dazed, barely noticing the white petals of a neighbor's row of honey locusts drifting to my head. I found my family in the kitchen and immediately reported my election.

"How did this happen?" My father looked vaguely puzzled. A Naval Academy graduate who served in the army, the only football game he cared about was Army vs. Navy, perhaps reflecting his lifelong question over which service he owed greater loyalty to. Friends considered his interest in only one game a distinction; football was the salt of everyday conversation in Gatesville. Civic duty practically demanded backing the high school team. Few of my father's friends attended the games; knowing the final score however, remained important. My father neglected even that. I suppose he either pretended to listen or somehow they forgave his ignorance because they saw him as a foreigner who'd settled in their midst. I knew only mild curiosity made him question.

Still shocked over my unexpected victory, I began to explain when my brother interrupted. "She jumped around in the gym and tore her clothes off. And when the principal told her to quit, she wouldn't."

Two years younger, he generally behaved as if I were invisible.

"Tore her skirt," Mother explained. "Caught her heels in the lace on the hem when she jumped."

She was provoked about this because she'd recently agreed I could buy the skirt made with lace showing under a ruffle, one of the many trends flouncing in and out of school during the year.

⊷ ⊷⊱ ⊶

The next September when players returned to school, Coach kept them busy working out all of the first weeks. Both A and B teams showed up to sit on the gym's bleachers in a large, silent clump—like visiting royalty watching the antics of the common people—at Friday afternoon pep rallies. The quarterback I had a crush on, looked more morose than the rest. A blonde boy with a strong jaw line, he seemed to be gritting his teeth at rallies. Slowly I discovered what everyone else already knew: Coach made the teams attend.

After pep rallies cheerleaders traditionally decorated the goal posts with crepe paper, one with the school's colors, black and yellow, a substitute for our unavailable gold. The opposite post we covered with the visiting team's colors. We spent hours before supper clinging with one hand to the goal posts, swaying back and forth on the school's one extra long ladder while telling each other what to do, and tossing tape back and forth. Those late afternoons spent wrapping the goal posts were, in retrospect, the best part of being a cheerleader; doing something totally unnecessary, which we fervently believed necessary. When the season gradually grew cooler, passing from summer to fall, long shadows fell across swaths of sunlight on the field. In the fading light, we grew quieter just before hurrying home. We'd set the stage; the ceremony could begin.

Before the first game, the previous year's two remaining cheerleaders showed us all the routines they knew. No one questioned where we acquired the cheers or made up any new ones; we did what was done before, what had probably been done ever since the school fielded a team.

"Okay," said the head cheerleader, the tallest one of us whose hair fell in bangs and curls around her long face, "let's do the locomotive."

All five of us knelt, and crooking our elbows, held each other's upper arms mimicking the machinery of a train. "You-rah-rah G.H.S.," we chanted louder and louder, faster and faster while jerking our arms in unison. It was as simple as the cheers we'd already learned before we tried out. I'd expected, after reading stories about cheerleaders and seeing pictures in magazines, we might learn more complicated maneuvers. But tumbling of any sort such as cartwheels, flips, or splits, was beyond us. No one mentioned pyramids. I felt I might attempt the cartwheel if I practiced, but how could I persuade the others to try, and how could we perform in white wool pleated skirts? Mother also pointed out the chances of catching a shoe's heel in the hem. When I despaired over our lack of proper training, my father said, "You might as well leave acrobatics to college cheerleaders," an especially hard-hearted comment as the Army and Navy teams had male cheerleaders.

Rules of pre-game etiquette were as uncomplicated as our cheers. To welcome the visiting cheerleaders, five of us held hands and ran across the football field in a line—the pep squad screaming as loud as it could in the stands behind us. Shortly before the opposing teams came on the field we introduced ourselves to the visitors, and told them we were looking forward to hearing their yells. They lied just as pleasantly. After the first game I realized we never heard exactly what the other side yelled.

Players didn't hear a word from either side. "It's noise, all noise," one said and grinned when he told me.

Right after the teams came out to take their positions for the first kick-off, one of the local preachers addressed the Almighty on the loudspeaker system. Standing under the lights, holding helmets by their sides, the boys, their close haircuts making them look vulnerable, bowed their heads. Stadium lights beamed down on all of us. The courthouse clock's deep gong, heard miles away, rang eight, and for a moment it was so quiet we could hear crickets chirping. On some nights I could hear them sizzling themselves on the big light bulbs during the silence of the pre-game prayer. Preachers varied, but the content of their prayers didn't. Good sportsmanship was invoked and many thanks given. As a drought crept toward us, they usually tacked on a plea for rain.

My duties remained the same for two years: We held pep rallies on Friday, wrapped the goal posts later that afternoon, and accompanied the team out of town—in the band bus. When I became head cheerleader the second year I kept a scrapbook. The school librarian told me it was my job now to make one although no one asked to see it, so every Saturday I cut out the weekly *Messenger's* straightforward version of the game. Its rival, the *County News,* largely dedicated to publishing the many opinions held by its editor—in badly-printed slightly smudgy type—didn't report on the games. Other than continual editorial columns, its content fell on the gossipy side. Two newspapers in a town of approximately 5,000 obviously needed at least one articulate malcontent; the *News's* editor served. A perpetually cross-looking man, his hands and clothes usually ink-smeared, he apparently enjoyed venting. Though his paper had fewer subscribers, at times he may have had more readers than the *Messenger.* Some of the cheerleaders were seen one Thursday night—without uniforms and therefore not performing officially— sitting in the back of a pickup moving slowly down Main chanting, "Wipe out Itasca!" and unrolling trails of toilet paper. The editor of the *County News* tattled.

"Couldn't you think of something else to shout?" Mother asked.

On Halloween, hidden by the drooping branches of a weeping willow tree on the lawn opposite, two majorettes, another cheerleader, and I held our giggles while four hulking football boys, backlit by a corner street light, hoisted an outhouse out of a pickup's bed and tiptoed to our American history teacher's yard. Her tough grading routinely threatened to force lazy students off the team. Tall, plain-faced, her gray hair braided and wrapped closely around her head, she provided a model of upright severity, one I gradually found admirable. Football players worried so about her standards they took her course in groups of three or four, as if they needed each other for protection. They paid the history teacher's power this honor every Halloween. She never remarked on the tradition; she simply called one of the majorettes' fathers who, with the help of a friend or two, returned the outhouse to the farmer missing one.

That week the *News's* editor noted in his usual orotund manner, "Four burley youths were discovered transporting a small house to the yard of a local teacher by moonlight." No names were recorded. Mother judged the *News's* editor a man of questionable taste. My father agreed, but insisted he published the real news.

I kept on clipping the *Messenger's* stories about the team's wins and losses. After the first two or three I quit reading. I still couldn't work up a true interest in slogging through week-old reports of football games, a traitorous lack I hid. I knew the meaning of phrases like "broken field running" and "flying tackle" and "quarterback sneak." I'd learned the basic rules of the game, but my interest remained half-hearted. Far more involved in writing for the school paper, rather like the

News's editor, I collected high school gossip, one sheet per week.

———※———

One Friday night, junior and senior girls played a Powder Puff game, the newest way someone thought might help raise funds for band uniforms. Two regular members of the team coached all of the Puffs for several afternoons. The quarterback I had a crush on, I was relieved to see, didn't volunteer to do any of the coaching. We used the boys' jerseys but decided not to wear pads since they made us look fat, nor would we wear helmets because they were too hot and turned our hair into sweaty wet strings. On game night the junior versus the senior girls threw themselves against each other resulting in furious stalemates, which took neither team much past the fifty-yard line and a zero to zero score. Sore shoulders, large bruises on our thighs, skinned elbows and the need to soak in hot baths resulted. At school the following Monday, feeling a certain familiarity about injuries, I stopped a regular team player in the hall to say I was sorry about the concussion he'd suffered two weeks previously.

He said, "Yeah...well, guess I'll live."

I could only nod. I wasn't as stoic, but if he wouldn't complain aloud I wouldn't either.

———※———

My junior year when I moved up to serve as head cheerleader, we acquired new uniforms; shorter black corduroy skirts, white sweaters featuring large black "Gs" and a gold one for me. The gold sweater—ordered by the faculty sponsor who said it was the nearest to a true gold she could find—was a disappointing pumpkin orange. Wearing it with my black skirt, I felt as if I had on a Halloween costume the whole season.

My mother's rule about accepting the first boy who asked for a date proved a worse disappointment. She knew I had to turn up at the annual Football Banquet and I wasn't dating anyone in particular at the time. Arranging my romantic interests to match my social needs was more than I could manage; usually I'd either just broken up with someone I'd lost all interest in, or someone lost interest in me, or I was longing for someone impossible like the quarterback. Because he called two weeks early, I had no choice: I had to go with the water boy. He was an inch or more shorter than I. At five feet, six inches, I couldn't overcome the height difference even by wearing flat heels and slumping. Thankful that banquets were spent sitting down, I thought probably he was too. Naturally we didn't talk about it. The things we didn't talk about were innumerable. Once the banquet was over, I sat in the water boy's family's car in front of my house, staring out the windshield thinking I'd rather liked him. He knew how to talk, how to say something beyond "Yeah" and "Naw." But, at last, a terrible silence slithered into the front seat like a large slice of black space that even our porch light couldn't penetrate.

"Thank you for taking me." I moved over closer and kissed him on the cheek.

He turned his head away then turned back to me. "Sometimes I see you out there, and I think you must be the only one really enjoying it."

"That's not true." I said, knowing when I did, the guilty freedom of confessing while still hiding my real feelings.

"I hate being water boy. Everybody thinks you're a wimp!" He put one of his hands on my right shoulder, pulled me forward, and kissed me.

Neither one of us was an expert; I shied so his mouth met mine in a lopsided way. I thought he looked relieved when we parted. The day after the banquet I went to classes wearing his letter jacket because of his insistence on following an unwritten rule kept by team members. By returning the jacket that afternoon, I canceled the rumor that we were going steady. Anyway, by that time, everyone knew I still had a crush on the quarterback who not only continued to ignore me, but also chose to go steady with a girl who lived so far out in the country I wondered when he saw her. She had to ride the school bus from her father's farm to town, but she went with the quarterback to the banquet and flaunted his letter jacket until spring when the weather got so hot she couldn't wear it.

Eventually my attention turned from that hopeless situation to a boy who had already graduated and gone to college. He came home on weekends often during his freshman year, and I was usually available.

The previous September, the school board had announced its decision to consolidate all the county's schools. All fall the quarterback's girlfriend had more company on the bus, as well as a majority of votes for cheerleader when spring election time came round again. After I congratulated her, the principal patted me on my back, and various teachers gave me sympathetic glances. Mortified, out of a job, and sure I was out of everyone's favor, I nodded and smiled at everyone until my cheeks ached before walking home alone surrounded by nature's mockery. The new leaves, the greening grass, and purple irises standing stiffly in their beds on everybody's lawn looked so full of promise, so terribly cheerful. By the time I got home, I threw myself across my own bed crying.

Mother came to the doorway of my room.

"I've just lost the cheerleader election, and there's a whole senior year ahead of me. What can I do?" Tears ran down my cheeks to drip on the bedspread.

"Can't you just go to school like everyone else?"

She was so reasonable I wailed louder.

My friends quickly gathered. Five of us crowded into a car and drove directly to a seldom-traveled dirt road where we rolled all the windows down and lit up. For several miles and cigarettes we used all of the limited number of curses we knew until one of the majorettes suggested, "You could join the band and still go to the out-of-town games with us."

"I can't join the band. I can't play anything."

They reminded me I'd taken piano lessons and could read music, which was true, although I read slowly. Then someone advised I try the lyre, "the thing with curls on top and horsetails dangling from either side. All you have to do is hang onto one of its top curls with one hand and bang on the notes with a little hammer with your other."

The next day I stayed after school to talk to the band director. He had red-blonde hair, which he was losing, freckles all over his arms, and a slightly worried frown on his pale freckled face. Known for his patience, he seemed to me to be someone who usually hid the pleasure of losing his temper but kept that privilege in mind.

"It's true a glockenspiel player will graduate this spring. Are you sure you want to try out? You'll have to come to band practice and you'll have learn to march."

I nodded. It was the first time I'd heard the lyre called a "glockenspiel."

His German pronunciation made it sound slightly exotic. He handed me a miniature book of sheet music, pointed to the alma mater, and asked me to play it for him before the band's rehearsal the following week.

Our alma mater had an easy melody and, like many a high school, 19th century sentiments. The first line went, "On Gatesville's fair horizon, reared against the sky, stands our faithful alma mater as the years go by." I'd sung it often before assemblies and games, but until I picked it out note for note on the glockenspiel, I hadn't paid much attention to its substance. Now I decided there was nothing particularly "fair" about the horizon. It was only rolling hill country flattening out to meet the west Texas plains. And I couldn't imagine an old two-story red brick building on top of a small rise "rearing," no matter how high the sky. "Alma mater" gave me trouble too. What did that Latin term really mean? I looked it up in the dictionary we used to settle arguments at home: "Fostering mother" was the translation. I refused to believe even in its context; though we had mainly women teachers, there was nothing motherly about high school. Nevertheless when I stood behind the stand with the glockenspiel's long, hairy white horses' tails hanging limply from either side and banged out the alma mater for the director, the years of practicing fake enthusiasm for football helped me play as though I loved every word and note of it. I was accepted as a band member immediately. There was one other glockenspiel player, a short plump girl, a year younger than I.

--- * ---

When band practice began in late August, heat did nothing to deter the director's desire for correct notes and straight rows. At first we practiced at night on the empty football field without instruments except for the drums rattling out march rhythms. After school began in September the heat continued, and we continued to march back and forth on the dual-purpose stadium grounds in new white cotton coveralls. Our feet killed the little grass left from July's rodeo. And though there were barely forty band members, a few quick turns swirled dust high enough to turn the new coveralls a powdery brown color, dark at the ankles, lighter as it reached our knees. Out in front of us, all of them dressed in cool white shorts and smart tasseled white boots, the majorettes pranced while cradling their batons in rigid crooks in their arms. Whenever the band stopped they twirled in flashy patterns practiced daily. Sweat trickled down my back. I caught much of the dust at the end of the last line as I stepped along sneaking glances at the glockenspiel player on the other end trying to keep even with her.

The director, also in coveralls, waved his arms and shouted, "Tighten those lines!" in a tired voice from his little foot-high director's stand on the sideline. One night after we'd finished and stood all dust-coated in formation before him, he announced, "Meet me at the band hall to pick up instruments tomorrow!"

The glockenspiel stood waiting on a stand. How was I to carry it? The other player showed me my harness, which had two V-shaped over-the-shoulder straps meeting in a narrow leather tube fitted to a short hollow pipe forming the instrument's base. Once I slipped into it, I found mine seemed to be designed to dig into my navel. This was not the only physical indignity. The director prized the new band uniforms which the other Powder Puffs and I had already helped buy with our bodies. These uniforms made of heavy wool serge durable enough to scratch for ten years, had mustard yellow high-necked jackets decorated with a double row of ball-shaped brass buttons. In back two short tails fell over black trousers. On our heads, we wore hats the same bright yellow as our jackets, with black patent visors and chinstraps. They looked a bit like French Foreign Legion kepis I'd seen in movies except, with all their braid, these were kepis no legionnaire would have worn.

In full uniform, covered from just below the chin to ankle in wool serge, topped by a too tight hat, carrying a heavy instrument hitting my navel while its horses' tails on either end swung in my face was torment. Dressing correctly and keeping in step was all I felt I could do. Why did our director believe we should also memorize all the notes to all the marches?

I played by ear. So did the other glockenspieler. After our first full-dress march down Main the Friday morning before the game, the director scolded. "You glockenspiel players! You sound like two chickens pecking away in the yard! You're supposed to play together!"

We nodded silently. The rest of the band waited in a clump, deaf to the name of any instrument except their own. Later my majorette friends were called to a closed-door conference where they were warned not to prance "so boldly."

"You would have thought he was talking to five sluts!"

Pleased with the "slut" idea, they refused to change their steps. The director might admonish them privately, but he wouldn't in public. They kept prancing.

It was a fairly good season for the Gatesville High School Hornets, but riding the band bus with the pep squad and new cheerleaders was not as much fun as I'd thought it would be. When I complained to my boyfriend, home from his college for the weekend, he reminded me he'd played the trumpet in the band himself for four years.

"You've got a great director. He knows how to play every one of those instruments, specially the winds, the French horn, the trumpet, the trombone, the tuba, the clarinet, the saxophone."

And when I added that the bus rides were boring, he laughed and said, "Yes, so is high school," in a disdainful tone. He'd given up the trumpet entirely, and after a year at his university, had decided to major in business. His life was taking shape; I was marching in place in mine.

All through the hot months of September and October our wool serge uniforms chafed and itched. By November freezing winds blew right through them. On game nights, in dread of the glockenspiel punching my navel, I began to have stomachaches before the games. Football season finished just in time for us to start practicing for the annual spring symphonic music contests. I quit the band.

The director looked on the positive side. "There aren't many symphony pieces that have glockenspiel parts," he said.

"No, I guess there aren't," I agreed, glancing without regret at the horsetails hanging lankly and the harness loosely coiled around one of the metal curls on top of the one I was leaving.

At the same time, I felt more than a little guilty. I'd never learned to hit all of anything correctly but the alma mater. As for the rest of the music, the other bad musician and I took turns playing by ear. If our director noticed, he said nothing. But if he'd heard both of us pecking away like chickens while we were marching down Main, I realized he knew we were still pecking, though one by one.

In part I felt grateful. He'd given me a way out, still I was unhappy. Toleration worked for the other player. She was sixteen. I was seventeen and a graduating senior.

"I never got to be a good glockenspiel player...not even half good. Thanks for letting me scratch around in the band though."

The director looked a little puzzled, flapped shut some sheet music he held, then smiled slightly. "Sure," he said. And with that one word, he released me to make my own more grievous, or more fortunate choices.

Sheep May Safely Graze

Next door to us in Gatesville, the small Texas town my family moved to after World War II, lived the Beasleys in a gaunt, unpainted frame house on an almost treeless corner. The house, stripped to its essentials, looked like something left after a hurricane or one of those hopeless, slightly-listing weathered gray houses in a ghost town. The Beasleys' house stood waiting, it appeared, for whatever further disaster might over take it. On its deep front porch Mr. Beasley sat wearing a clean shirt, suspenders holding up a rumpled pair of pants of no distinguishable color, and his faded brown felt hat. Tilted back against the gray wall in a thin-slatted wooden chair, he smoked his pipe and talked to Mrs. Beasley who was just as badly clothed in a faded cotton dress that loosely covered her body. She had a pleasant face and smiled readily, but she was undeniably fat; her flesh hung on her arms in loose pillows; her stomach rose in her lap when she sat down.

The renovated, freshly-painted gray bungalow with white trim and a wrap-around front porch next door to the Beasleys' was ours. On the other side of us stood another bungalow, slightly smaller, painted gray-blue with a porch only in front. The people who lived there were civil; they came and went sharing an alleyway entrance to their garage with us, waving or nodding when they saw us. Their one memorable act was to cut down a storm-damaged cedar elm and turn the remaining three-foot stump into a base for a birdbath. I had little interest in them.

Raised near two Civil War battlegrounds, constantly told about the generations preceding my own, I had some conscious sense of history. The Beasleys' house, to my way of thinking, was left over from some vaguely earlier time, to the years long before I arrived in Gatesville, before there were many paved roads, before zoning laws, or even, perhaps, before streets were laid out. Their house could have once been a farmhouse with a well in back and a fence to keep livestock out.

I said nothing to my parents about these assumptions. The town was full of remnants of the Old West: wooden awnings sheltering storefronts on Main Street, hitching posts, people who remembered the last public hanging outside the courthouse on the square in the twenties, now and then the clip-clop sound of shoes made by people riding horseback on the streets, and an annual rodeo and rodeo parade every summer. Men wearing cowboy hats and boots could be seen everywhere; my new stepfamily consisted partially of two ranching uncles who wore the same. Though they had been there a while, I couldn't see the Beasleys as figures from a cowboy movie come alive. There was nothing particularly western or in the least dashing about their clothing. They were only different and except for their obvious need, their lives were, to me, a continuing mystery.

A silently agreed upon veil, a refusal to be too nosey, generally falls between next-door neighbors. It had fallen at my grandmother's two-story gray brick house in Nashville where I'd lived during the war. At her home, only five or six feet from the red brick house next door, we spoke to the neighbors infrequently when we happened to glimpse them through the branches of maple trees dividing our front porches.

One afternoon an elderly man sitting on the porch coaxed a squirrel to scrabble up his pants legs and sit on his lap to eat peanuts.

I called through the branches. "Will he let you pet him?"

The elderly man said, "Not yet." and continued feeding the squirrel as if he held a squirrel in his lap every day of his life.

I ran back in our house to ask for peanuts, but we didn't have any, and, no, we weren't going to buy peanuts to feed squirrels that might bite children.

In the Beasleys' case, no division existed between us other than a wire fence made of small squares, the kind, I learned, generally used in the country to keep goats from straying. Fifty or sixty feet away, our neighbors were obviously there and, at the same time, shielded. My bedroom windows overlooked two of their west windows, but poor as they were, they had roller shades that neither a twelve-year-old girl peering through her Venetian blinds, nor anyone else could ever see through. In those pre-air-conditioned times, the first summer we lived next door they opened one shade and one window to reveal a kitchen where I could see Mrs. Beasley puttering about while her husband sat at the table under a cartoon-like single dangling light bulb. I couldn't determine exactly what either one of them was doing, but obviously they had a kitchen and used it just as everyone did. A stove and refrigerator gleamed vaguely in the murky interior.

In plain view of all the neighborhood, three nameless black-faced sheep wandered the Beasleys' backyard, mowing it closely and leaving their black oval dung to fertilize the ground, a lawn-keeping method my father admired until he noticed Mr. Beasley raked a path through the backyard every Saturday so Mrs. Beasley wouldn't have to step on the homemade fertilizer Monday morning. On Sundays the sheep grazed in the wire-fenced front yard while Mr. Beasley read a copy of *The Dallas Morning News* someone must have given him. It took him most of the day to read it.

There was something jaunty about Mr. Beasley, some devil-may-care hint in his eyes, a slightly cocky slant to his felt hat. But Mrs. Beasley was in bad health though the kind of trouble she had was never defined. I thought, in addition to some unnamed illness, she must have suffered from the weather. She never wore anything but sleeveless dresses my mother called "shifts." We saw Mrs. Beasley more often on Mondays when she hung the wash out. Her thin, loose dress showed a second pillow of fat high on each arm. No matter how cold it was, she appeared outside, reaching to fasten clothespins to a wire line while her dress—pale green or blue—flapped around her. Just the sight of her on a November day made me shiver. In the late spring sometimes she would sit out on the front porch next to Mr. Beasley, her round face framed by gray curls. Mr. Beasley waved to anyone passing by, but Mrs. Beasley ventured only a nod.

"Oh, there's Mrs. Beasley." Mother usually announced in a voice half-pitying, half reproachful. She called not only her close friends but the majority of the people she knew, by their first names, and she knew nearly everyone since she'd lived in Gatesville most of her adult life. Reversing the rule I'd known, Mr. and Mrs., I learned, were usually reserved for the yardman, the wives of the men who'd worked for her, anyone down a notch on her social scale, and of course new people she'd recently met. We had moved there just after my parents married. Mother was the only native Texan in our family. She had her own horse, her own car, her own ranch, and a Texaco wholesale gasoline business which, after running it during World War II with the help of another woman and "an old man with a bad back," she turned over to my father. As a newcomer alert to the differences in people's lives in Gatesville, a town so unlike the southern places I'd known, I listened carefully to the tone of her voice. The Beasleys were, I gathered in a half-knowing adolescent way, lower on her scale, but their poverty wasn't the only determining factor. It was the sheep, I thought, the shifts, and the fact that Mr. Beasley, obviously in good health, didn't have any kind of job, nor did he seem to want one. Many people in town were wavering between getting by and getting better then. Because of the proximity of Fort Hood, the town had endured the war years well, but when the war was over and the troops went home, post-war prosperity crawled slowly into Gatesville. Our purchase of the renovated bungalow was part of it. When we first got to town we'd lived in a little rent house, some of my clothes were Mother's cut down to my size, and trips to a new orthodontist in the nearest city had to wait. Both my brother and I had lived with relatives for four war years. I'd never seen Mother wear the skirts she had made over for me, and I didn't miss the braces or the orthodontist. I did notice how small the rent house was. I missed my grandmothers' houses, one large two-story gray brick with ample rooms, another a two-storied Victorian with porches on three sides. I missed the old, well-known amplitude of those houses, familiar places in familiar country. But I didn't mind being poor in Gatesville any more than the Beasleys seemed to. I knew we were beginning again.

My father had a strong belief in western egalitarianism as opposed to his better-known, stratified southern world. There were the poor, then our own middle class as everyone claimed to be, although we were well aware there was an upper class composed of new rich and old. Old money was best of all. Education, hard work and merit slid people up while lack of any of these could force them down. Kinfolk, of course, escaped all categories. Naturally such stratification was seldom mentioned; it was absorbed through one's pores, mine as well as my father's—plus he'd known the absolute hierarchy of the army. By remarrying and moving west, he felt he'd escaped the South. Of course war's end allowed him to escape the military, in part, but only in part. Men who have graduated from military academies and served in long campaigns don't escape that easily. In fact, while he was still in his late forties, he was offered the rank of general if only he'd return, but he'd had enough of the service. Like some of his friends who were also veterans, his favorite everyday uniform was a pair of khaki trousers and a matching khaki shirt with darker triangles and circles or half circles showing where insignia had been ripped off. Despite my father's dream of civilian equality, Mr. Beasley called him "Colonel" every time he saw him. Mother hewed to "Mr. and Mrs. Beasley."

I didn't truly know how Mr. Beasley occupied himself. He had a son, I'd heard, a retired army officer, who sometimes telephoned. Mr. Beasley would announce when he'd received a call, but we never saw his son in Gatesville. I wondered if perhaps Mr. Beastly might be ill himself in some unnoticeable way. Though they had no car he was fit enough, however, to walk to town; he also walked to the post office to pick up social security checks and those his son sent him, we surmised. I decided his son must have also been the one who sent him the Sunday paper.

After we'd lived there a while, I discovered that Mr. Beasley was one of Gatesville's old men designated as a "courthouse loafer." They assembled on the steps of the courthouse, a magnificent nineteenth-century pile of creamy limestone with windows and doors outlined in red sandstone where two larger-than-life figures of Justice holding the scales stood above both east and west pediments. The loafers met everyday on the north side, out of sight of the justices, and from this point they collected gossip and kept up with city and county politics. I supposed they knew everything going on in Gatesville, but my father insisted they knew nothing but the most flagrant hearsay. They trafficked in rumor and guesswork, which amused my father so much he would sometime check on their conversation. Afterward he'd come home and report the more sensational parts to Mother who deplored his interest but did listen. Mr. Beasley, from her point-of-view, also specialized in irritating comment.

When she decided to change the looks of the front porch by replacing its stubby half-pillars with taller white wrought-iron standards so many people were fond of in the fifties, Mr. Beasley announced in passing, "You're ruining the best part of that house!"

"Now how would he know!" she fumed.

Some days, during my father's rare attempts at gardening, he talked to Mr. Beasley over the side fence separating their large barren lot from the tidy beds of nandina and iris bordering ours. Cedar elms and oaks also flourished in our front and backyards while the Beasleys had only one small drooping chinaberry tree growing up against the east side of their house. The sheep quietly cropped grass behind Mr. Beasley while he talked. Even when the grass was so low it was barely visible; the black-faced sheep appeared fat and healthy.

Mother may not have totally approved of Mrs. Beasley's shifts, but she always spoke to her when they both happened to be outside hanging clothes on their lines. The sheep, however, were a great annoyance. She waved her hand in front of her nose while my father argued for neighborly acceptance and the intelligent, utilitarian use of browsing animals.

Knowing she couldn't get him to agree, Mother could only sigh. Mr. Beasley, after one of his early conversations with my father, let it be known he had an arrangement with someone who hauled the sheep away twice a year. December through February and June through August, they disappeared, so Mother could look forward to some relief.

Whatever was needed to change the Beasleys' way of life did not happen. The military son never swooped in to be shocked over the house's naked need of stronger framework and paint. Mrs. Beasley's shifts were not replaced for something more suitable for a woman her age in cold weather, and the sheep continued to graze the backyard for at least six months of every year. I gradually grew accustomed to the Beasleys and their sheep. Among all of us who were striving one way or another—to grow up, to better ourselves, to improve the town—they went on as before—silently ailing, at rare times cantankerous, continually impoverished, getting by in their gaunt house.

In a few years I went away to college and came back home to marry. In early June, before it got too hot, my parents decided to hold the reception in our backyard. Mother mentioned aloud that though she'd long ago given up on them ever getting a paint job, she hoped the Beasleys' sheep would vanish on schedule.

Carried along by waves of exciting necessities such as taking my last finals, graduating, and marrying, dazed by my own self-importance, I was only vaguely conscious of her worries.

My father, in an effort to help, had planted at least a hundred white gladioli which were appearing erratically, poking their heads one by one above ground to bloom too early. The florist had to be alerted to order more. Instead of using someone local, I'd hired a photographer from Austin who Mother neither knew nor was inclined to trust, and there was no really good motel in Gatesville to house our out-of-town guests. Worst of all, my father had become president of the Chamber of Commerce. In that dry town we would be traitors if we spiked the punch or offered champagne toasts. I particularly regretted the loss of the champagne. Midst these concerns, my father laughed and reminded Mother the sheep wouldn't be seen even if they were still in residence the second week in June. It would almost be dark by the time guests arrived.

Waving her hand in front of her nose, she was not altogether reassured. At her insistence, I was sent to the Beasleys' front door to deliver a wedding invitation by hand. The wedding date might help remind them, since it seemed they had forgotten, that it was time to ship the sheep to summer pasture.

Standing on the Beasley's porch under its weak light, I had time to see inside their splintery screen door before Mr. Beasley answered. There was nothing on the opposite wall but a bit of yellowed wallpaper that had turned brown around the edges.

When Mr. Beasley shuffled up to me, I handed him the heavy, cream-white envelope, chosen for its dignified weight, holding the engraved invitation. He looked much the same, old as he had always been but with a definitely interested gleam in his eyes. We'd long ago mailed the others that all included an invitation to the reception at our house following the wedding, so I told the white lie Mother and I had agreed on.

"Since we're neighbors, I waited till I got home from school to bring this over."

The minute I said it, guilt overwhelmed me. Such a shabby lie. Why couldn't we have thought of something better? Why couldn't one of us have gone over and simply asked Mr. Beasley if he was going to send the sheep away before the party? Although Mother had already reminded me that there were plenty of other courtesy invitations to people who wouldn't come, I felt it was particularly hypocritical to ask next door neighbors to a wedding three days before the date when we knew she had only shifts to wear, and he had never been seen in a suit. Standing in front of Mr. Beasley, I decided I didn't care. What difference would it make if they came suitless and in a shift, the way they dressed for their lives? The sheep didn't matter either. I wanted to blurt out all this but feared whatever I said might sound insulting. Even in the egalitarian West, how can a person say politely, I don't care if you keep sheep. It doesn't matter if you're poor and dress funny. Please come to my wedding anyway. I waited bound by the ancient ritual, which makes two people silently agree to accommodate each other.

Mr. Beasley stared at me a bit longer before saying, "I heard you were getting married."

Usually happy to talk about the attributes of my husband-to-be and our plans for the future, now overcome by what I should have done and said, at first I could only nod dumbly. Then, in hopes of saying something encouraging, I added, "If you can't come to the wedding, maybe you'll come to the reception." Once it was said, I realized how cutting it might sound to Mr. Beasley and immediately felt shame descending on me as though it were beamed down from his porch light.

He tapped the unopened invitation against his palm, cocked his head, and said, "Thank you."

Two days later the sheep were gone.

As expected the Beasleys didn't come to the wedding or the reception but they left a gift at our front door, a small copper-bottomed saucepan, definitely a useful object which, except for polishing now and then, required no up-keep.

We were moving out of state, and all my thank-you notes were tardy except for the one written to the Beasleys. Exactly what I wrote I've forgotten, however I did say something about what good neighbors they had always been.

They have been gone for many years now, and so have I. The last time I was in Gatesville I drove past the bungalow that used to be ours to discover the Beasleys' gray ruin had been replaced by a small white frame house, one without the slightest portent of disaster or a single sheep to mow the lawn. Gazing at this ordinariness, I wished for the Beasleys sitting on their porch again, waving and nodding, maintaining their dignity, keeping their mysterious lives to themselves as usual while their sheep browsed the continually growing grass.

My Father's Guns

My father was forbidden by his mother to bring a gun into the house. She had deep convictions against guns, almost as deep as those her religion held against drinking. Regardless of her disapproval, my grandfather made wine in the basement during Prohibition, but in one of those paradoxes familiar to families, he stood by her when she insisted that the commandments totally forbade killing. So young William Culbert never brought a gun in the house. However, when he was fourteen, his mother's own father, Isaac Newton Phillips, whose very name indicated a wider point of view, bought him a shotgun and took him bird hunting in the fields near Nashville, those farms and pastures out of town thick with hedgerows, stone fences, and weeds surrounding fields where coveys of quail might hide. There was perhaps a relative or friend who had one of those places where hunters waited on the edge of a wood before walking slowly out, watching sharply for the slightest rustle in the grass. Preferably they walked with a pointer quartering the field before them, waiting for the dog to pick up the distinctive quail scent and grow "birdie," a continual quivering shudder of controlled nervous energy rippling through Judy's or Lucy's or Queenie's liver-spotted hide, before she froze in the classic one-paw uplifted stance. Then Grandpa Phillips, in a soft voice, would command, "Steady! Hold steady!" They would walk forward until the birds flushed, choosing the one bird each would aim for. As the air filled with the wing-beating rushing noise of quail rising, their guns rose almost simultaneously to spray the shot in its somewhat inexact yet lethal killing pattern.

"Grandpa was the best wing shot I ever knew," my father said. The old man's insistence on shooting birds only as they rose in the sky in flight toward safety, toward life, was, he implied, the only fair way.

"What's so fair about it?" my mother asked later, adding her disapproval to Grandmother's interdiction. None of it would have happened if he hadn't taken a weapon to the field. What, beside flight, was a bird's weapon?

Her question was never fully answered. There was some talk of the erratic movement of birds in flight, their speed, their natural camouflage, but Mother's notion of fairness was, to my father, merely a sentimental female response, and had to his way of thinking, nothing to do with the sport. The right way, the way things were supposed to be done by men hunting, captured his attention.

The dog, if she were a good one, would find the dead birds. Holding them lightly in her mouth, she would bring them one by one, to the hunters. Their warmth, the quickness of life giving over to the suddenness of death, never failed to move my father, but it didn't keep him from wringing a bird's neck if life lingered. It was also the rule of the hunt, and I believe, a long-held wish for the quick death he wanted for himself.

My father always used female pointers, an irony he refused to admit. Mother so consistently referred to this habit that it became a worn-out comment, a mere cliché used by a woman. A generation later I let that irony slide. By then so much had happened—World War II, its atomic ending, Korea, Vietnam—the sex of a hunting dog was a small matter, a small irony. I grew up accustomed to being the daughter of a father who hunted and fished. Our fireplace in the first house we lived in was furnished with gray and white birch bark logs he'd brought home from one of his fishing trips to Canada. Those logs were never burned, and I think of them now as emblematic of a desire for wilderness, heavily forested, barely populated land where my father and his friends, often as many as six other men, lived near the water, portaging their canoes as they followed the veins winding among islands and lakes for weeks. There are pictures, little sepia-toned, two by three-inch snapshots with the ornamental borders used in the 1930s, made by one of his friends when they camped. Some of them are the usual ones of men in long underwear, the fish caught, and campsites but others show men doing chores; shaving, washing dishes, washing their clothes, and most of the time the washer is grinning as if he were saying, "Yes, I can do this too. I can take care of my own necessities." Years later when I was teaching Hemingway's fishing stories, Nick Adams prepared his supper of canned pork and beans, spaghetti, tomato ketchup, bread, and finished it off with canned apricots and coffee after carrying it all day in his heavy pack. One of the few things he said aloud was, "I have a right to eat this kind of stuff if I'm willing to carry it." I thought then of those Canadian snapshots and recognized my father's and his friends' pride in their self-sufficiency. When I collected those pictures in a scrapbook for him, he looked at each one carefully and laughed a little ruefully as if remembering something he'd almost forgotten.

Those trips didn't end altogether, but they were curtailed in the years following the Depression, especially those after his wedding in 1933. "When your mother married," I was told by one of my father's sisters, "she had five tea gowns in her trousseau...those long, drifty dresses women sometimes changed into around four or five in the afternoon. And Brother took her off to some kind of fishing lodge for their honeymoon."

I wondered how long it took my mother to realize she needn't unpack those gowns. I know the cocktail hour soon replaced teatime, for whatever else they packed and portaged, those fishermen carried whisky. In that tribe, drinking was almost as time-honored as the sport itself. During the Canadian trips, they grew tired of eating fish, but that was the other necessary half of it; whatever was killed had to be eaten and this was equally true of hunting. Whether it was duck hunting on frozen Reelfoot Lake in Tennessee or antelope hunting in West Texas, we ate whatever my father brought home, and in the days before home freezers were widely available, we ate game soon after it arrived. This was true in my grandmother Culbert's house as well. She forbade guns, but whatever was killed was eaten. My Scotch-Irish grandfather Culbert was only one generation removed from the famine and to him wasting food was a greater sin than killing. My family ate wild duck for Christmas dinner, usually served with a glass of the vinegar-flavored Prohibition wine Grandfather had concocted. The Christmas I was allowed a taste I was, for once, thankful to be a child. Frog legs, quail, and dove, were all, at various times, also available. When we moved to Texas, the wild game list broadened to include venison, antelope, and much later, pheasant. Quail and dove were nearest, therefore the most often hunted. We often talked about how to cook possum, javelina, and armadillo, but these native curiosities never reached our table.

The way the light played on the leaves, the abstruseness of some dogs who failed to fetch correctly, the clarity or cloudiness of the sky as the birds rose against it—all of these the hunters took in, recounted as they recounted the number of coveys startled. But once the limit was reached, or darkness fell, the cleaning began. Cold running water helped scour out cavities made by knives used to remove heads and guts. Then the birds were plucked. As a young girl I couldn't understand how they could throw away all those beautiful feathers; nevertheless, the hunters let the wind take some and the rest were delivered to the garbage. None of the women in the family ever helped pluck game birds. We would carefully search them for shot before cooking, but the right way of hunting, the way Great-Grandpa Phillips taught my father, required the killer to clean his game.

Why didn't my father's father, my Grandfather Culbert, become a hunter? A city man, already grown by the time Great-Grandpa Phillips knew him, he was a boilermaker, son of an Irish immigrant boilermaker, not a man inclined to hunt, though he was willing for his son to learn. Was it a matter of some inherited idea of class? Did hunting belong only to the landed gentry? That couldn't be true. Great-Grandpa Phillips was a roofing contractor himself. But perhaps my grandfather felt a tinge of workingman's prejudice. I'd rather believe it was lack of interest as well as lack of time. He had a partnership in a factory owned with a brother. They employed three or four other men and worked with them to make those Medusa-headed metal machines where soft coal and boiling water supplied heat for a house's radiators. By 1946, the "Big Inch" pipelines wriggling from East Texas through Tennessee, and on north, constructed during the war, opened to furnish natural gas. All our lives changed the same year.

All our lives changed long before then. My father divorced and married my stepmother who was from Texas. She lived in a little town called Gatesville, named after Ft. Gates, an old frontier army fort.

We moved to Gatesville, and among the many things we brought with us was his gun collection, including the heavy Kentucky flintlock, a long rifle with brass designs of diamonds and a heart on its stock, the gun one of Great-Grandpa Phillips's ancestors supposedly carried over the Cumberland Gap when he came to settle in Tennessee. It was a romantic view of a family's past and a highly satisfactory one, built on the mere existence of the gun. No one remembered the original owner, so we were free to believe what we pleased. I imagined it riding on the shoulder of a tall, weary man as he climbed through the dark Appalachian forest. He had to push himself through the steep gap first found by Thomas Walker's exploring party, and later blazed by Daniel Boone when he was making his Wilderness Road, the same road that nearly 200,000 others took between 1775 and 1800. Union armies would use it to invade Tennessee in 1862 and 1863. The ancestral gun rested in storage, deposited in Nashville with his other belongings, until my father retrieved it to carry to his new home, though not on his shoulders. The gun traveled, ingloriously crated with others, to Texas where it would hang in my brother's bedroom. It hangs now in my own living room in Austin, waiting to be passed on to my son and his sons. To me it's a reminder of my own family's and this country's westward movement.

My father remained a hunter even during World War II. After graduating from Annapolis, serving in the navy three years, quitting the service, working for a year in New York, marrying, holding a job in Nashville, and fathering two children, he was thirty-eight in 1941. His life took a different turn after Pearl Harbor. He could go on duty with the navy, which offered him two weeks to settle his affairs and an assignment at sea immediately.

Because he'd already spent five years as a training officer in the National Guard, the army offered him all the time he wanted, a first post near Nashville, and a promised rise in rank to Lt. Colonel in the field artillery. I was too young to notice the agonies of indecision this must have caused him. He saved his Annapolis peacoat, his diploma, his officer's sword, his 1925 dress uniform including the tailcoat, gold epaulets, and cocked hat, all kept in a succession of attics, and chose the army. By the time the army moved him to California, he was already in charge of training battalions of anywhere from 500 to 1,200 men. He volunteered for combat—men were anxious to fight in that war when good and evil were so clearly defined. But those in command asked him to stay in California to train other soldiers. Gradually he learned to endure the special guilt of the man who stays behind while the men he's prepared go off to war.

On weekends later in the war he sometimes went hunting. Long after WWII was over I found a black and white picture of him standing in a field, palm trees in the background, and he's looking down at a spotted pointer, one I didn't know. When I first saw it, I was as dismayed as my Grandmother might have been. Why would anyone even dream of shooting a gun for recreational purposes when there was a war on?

I've never been able to find a complete answer for this. At first it seemed a bloody-minded thing to do, one of those contrarieties of human nature that will prevail in spite of commonsense, in spite of the pragmatic streak shown by his choice of army over navy, in spite

of a professed hatred of war, and a profound weariness
with the subject when it was over.

I wasn't around at every stage of his life, but I saw
him cry only once. He sat in the middle of a couch at
my maternal grandmother's house in Franklin and wept
openly at the news of the attack on Pearl Harbor. I can't

Carolyn and her father, Lt. Col William Culbert,
home on leave, 1944.

remember exactly why we were there or who else was in the room except my mother sitting next to him. I can't remember running to him or trying to comfort him in any way. I can't even remember whether or not Mother also cried. I stood as still as a seven-year-old could and watched, shocked into silence by the tears running unchecked down his cheeks.

He wasn't crying, I'm sure, because he would have to report for duty. The years of military education followed by three years at sea plus time given later to help form the Tennessee National Guard had trained him well. Duty was one of his sacred words. He cried, I think now, because having practiced preparedness for years, he was still surprised by the attack and furious about our country's complete lack of readiness for it. In the warfare he'd studied, no one had used ships to launch planes as the Japanese did.

Later during the war, he must not have made a connection between training men to kill other men and killing animals for sport. In his mind, I suppose, the two were always divided. In the picture he is wearing civvies; perhaps he found hunting a brief return to his civilian life, a holiday from the army just as, during the first part of the war when we had joined him in California, he gathered his family from the hotel where we were living and took us for two days to a real house close to a beach where we swam and built sand castles and the roar of the waves drowned out all mention of conflict. We were sent home in 1942 when he realized it was going to be a long war, so his dependents were not a distraction any more. He had another. Following a dog while cradling a borrowed shotgun was a long way from loading a howitzer, a long way from teaching surveying, replacement, alignment, and the multitude of other details he trained men to attend to. Hunting and fishing had long been his choices of leisure occupation. While a civilian he didn't play golf or tennis and though he'd jumped hurdles for the Annapolis track team, he had no regular exercise program other than walking the fields in the fall and early winter. Hunting and fishing were his passions; as he grew older, they remained instinctive reactions, a way to relieve his mind of the tedium of business, to concentrate attention on something other than certain large griefs he had, and above all, to get out in the infinitely more interesting natural world.

During the last part of the war, when stationed at South Ft. Hood, Texas, and still training soldiers, he took a whole company of around 200 men to the nearest lake on a fishing trip as a reward for proving themselves battle ready. They camped out in army tents on the banks of the lake and went bass fishing. Surely some of them just slept; otherwise they would have fished the lake empty in a weekend.

Once peace was declared and we were all in Texas, my ten-year-old brother was trained to hunt at our stepmother's ranch. Though we were both usually jealous of the amount of attention either of us could capture from a re-acquired father, I wasn't in the least interested in learning how to shoot, nor at twelve, did I want to follow my father and brother around when they left to practice.

Perhaps my stepmother's memory of a deer hunt in South Texas influenced me. During a winter when she was younger, she'd been stationed high in an oak tree.

"A group of deer stepped out to look for acorns just below. They were beautiful, so beautiful I just couldn't shoot. I just sat there holding my breath and watching them…two does, a fawn, and a six point buck."

I could see her there camouflaged behind the tree's evergreen leaves staring down at the deer, their coats a golden brown, the fawn's lighter brown coat spotted with white, waiting as they delicately bent to eat, while she withheld an eminent death.

"I've never hunted since," she said.

My father would shake his head and grin when she recited this incident.

We didn't have deer at the ranch then. Hungry early settlers had killed all the native herds by 1900. About seventy years later they began to drift back from less settled parts of Texas to our country.

In those earlier days, after being cautioned to look out for rattlesnakes, I walked off in a direction safely distant from the gun practice to climb the low mesas, to explore this new territory of scrubby brush, cedar, mesquite, huizache, pecans, live oak, elm, Mexican plum. I might happen across hidden springs or arrowheads. If I were lucky, I might scare up a jackrabbit or an armadillo skittering toward its hole. I didn't go hunting with my father until I was married and he'd begun teaching my husband who'd grown up on the nearly treeless Texas Panhandle's High Plains—that part of the country Coronado called the Staked Plains—where he'd hunted foxes, coyotes, and rabbits. Though pheasant were successfully established in the sixties, it wasn't deer or quail country. Thousands of migrating ducks and geese landed on shallow playa lakes—if there had been enough rain to fill them. Doves flew in from the north, but no one in his family used a shotgun.

Dove hunting season begins in Central Texas around September first when we're usually nearing the end of a summer's drought, and the temperature remains in the 90s, too high to enjoy being outside long. Hiding behind the earthen bank of one of the ranch's tanks, the men wait for sundown when birds fly to water. There is, as a practical matter, no use for a bird dog then. While the weather is so hot rattlesnakes are still slithering around, a bird dog, anxious to hunt, will run through the fields oblivious to any danger. My father's pointer, who'd begun whimpering when he began cleaning his gun on the back patio, was left at home until most of the snakes kept to their dens in colder weather.

Our son, when he was seven and still too young to have a gun, began to wait with his grandfather. He stood beside him when he fired and collected his shell casings; some of those eventually made their way into pieces of complicated castles he built with colored blocks. Chiggers and mosquitoes preyed on the hunters; heat was omnipresent. The western sun behind their backs gave them a slight advantage as they hunkered on the caliche nubby with small fossils shoved out of the ground by a bulldozer to form the tank's high bank where one old mesquite was allowed to stay mainly because it had always been there. Just as the sun fell below the horizon, the birds were sharply profiled as they flew toward the water. But some Septembers were still too hot to interest even the most avid hunters, and in some others early rains made a tank an unnecessary water supply. Then the old recipes handed from mothers to daughters or from hunter to hunter went unused.

I didn't care to sit and wait for birds to fly to a water hole during a hot, dry twilight. I waited for the cooler days of the quail season, around November first here, to walk the fields with my father and my husband. When the grasses had been bleached light brown and the little bluestem and taller Indian grass evolved into red swathes across the pastures repeating the color of red oak leaves, we were all glad of the release from the air-conditioned caves we'd lived in all summer. Then Queenie, my father's last pointer, would work in front of us, quivering with repressed eagerness to hear his order, "Find the birds!" and once it was given, to dash wildly ahead, nose to the ground. She'd hold a point, wait until the quail were flushed, wait still frozen while the men fired, then retrieve the dead birds only after repeated commands between making forays to find more.

My father shouted her name until he was almost hoarse then used an old brass army whistle to call her. Sometimes neither was effective. Queenie's genes compelled her to hunt, however no amount of training or pleading could make her follow all of the hunt's ancient pattern. There are stories about hunters losing their tempers and trying to discipline dogs by peppering them with birdshot from a distance close enough to sting, far enough not to kill the dog. My father never shot Queenie or any of his dogs though his own temper was often unreliable. I asked him once how he was able to keep from firing at her. His reply was, "Too dangerous. You can ruin a dog that way." And, obviously, he loved his dogs.

When the day's hunt was over my father took a drink, bourbon or vodka, straight from the bottle he carried with him. Sometimes he took more than one, a habit his wife deplored. He'd had two heart attacks, she argued, and there were thirty miles to drive home from the ranch, on an uncrowded road; still there were other people's lives to consider. He may have considered them; he wouldn't give up liquor. If someone went hunting with him, they drank with him, even my young husband did, and he'd been charged to look after his father-in-law. Drinking after a hunt, never before, was a ritual as well as a habit.

I'm sure it was the same when he hunted with other men although there wasn't one particular group as his earlier fishing friends had been. His hunting friends were solitary ranchers, often veterans, who invited him to come to their places. He always went and he went alone. Such invitations were the best compliments he could possibly receive. At times they were also debts he couldn't repay exactly as he could never offer antelope, and deer didn't return to Central Texas till soon after he died in 1968. He knew they were on the way, however; he'd found evidence of a place one had bedded down while he was out quail hunting the previous fall.

After his death from a sudden heart attack—he'd planned a fishing trip the next day—Queenie lived for several years more as my mother's slightly distant companion. My father never wanted us to make a household pet of his hunting dog. In fact the only time his dog was ever in the house was for a few minutes on Christmas Day when a ceremonial red bow was tied around her collar and she came in to slide nervously over the hardwood floor, her nails clicking as she tried furiously for a foothold. The dog was relieved to return to her pen, and we were just as relieved to let her go. A hunting dog belonged outside in a pen. Bringing one inside, cosseting it in any way would, my father believed, spoil the dog's eagerness to hunt. When we first came to Texas we owned an Irish setter that my brother and I ruined, my father often said, by making a pet of him. We were sure he put off training the dog until too late. And we were equally certain the one male hunting dog he'd owned—the best natured, most handsome dog we ever had with a setter's usual lustrous dark rust-colored coat— was simply dumb. To an extent, our father agreed. Rusty repeatedly caught his head in his pen's fence at night and howled till someone came out to turn his head enough to let him pull it back through. He lost his way home when he escaped our yard for a ramble and was ignominiously confused by an automatic door that trapped him in a neighbor's garage. Rusty would have been easier to discipline, our father argued, if he'd been petted only briefly in passing. And instead of lazing round the back yard waiting for us to come home from school, he should have been left to live in his pen.

My stepmother naturally continued to feed and water his last dog, the one that never hunted again. And she would let Queenie out of her pen often to run in the walled backyard, but between them there wasn't much show of affection, though I felt they both remained steadfast to different memories of the same man.

Because my brother died young, and our stepmother no longer wanted them, I inherited my father's guns. He'd kept them in two pine cabinets built on either side of his bed's headboard. Though the apparently Freudian significance of their location seemed obvious, it was too obvious. We lived in a renovated three-bedroom bungalow, and Mother was not about to allow guns in the living or dining rooms. The hall was too small for cabinets; furniture took up all the space in my brother's room and in mine. The only room left was my parents' bedroom, already over-filled with a serpentine fronted mahogany suite, another gift to my father from his Grandpa Phillips who had no other grandsons, no one else to teach to hunt.

Opposed to the gun cabinets in the bedroom from the beginning, my stepmother insisted that we empty them. But what were we to do with seventeen guns in our small house where we lived with three small children? For a month we literally slept on them; all seventeen were hidden in their cases under our bed. We had no attic, no other safer place to put guns, and we didn't want the children to see them. They looked for monsters under their own beds, but we wanted to believe they wouldn't look under ours. We couldn't afford to buy gun cabinets then. Also we soon became aware that though my husband still liked to hunt, we weren't going to display those guns, and we had no real need of them. Seventeen was an excessive number. We saved seven and sold the rest to a local gun shop. When we moved to a new house the long rifle was mounted under the mantle. A Charles Daly shotgun with Damascus double barrels made in Germany—in the part then called Prussia— at the end of the nineteenth century, the one left to my father by Great-Grandpa Phillips, was hidden in a secret storage place where we also stashed the silver when we went out of town. Next to it we laid a 1930s Fox shotgun my father probably bought himself. Though neither man stinted on good quality, these were utilitarian guns, not collectors' prizes. My father's army .45 revolver was tucked away in a shoebox up in a closet out of reach. His last shotgun, a 12 gauge Remington automatic, his deer rifle, a Remington 30.06, and his .22 caliber varmint rifle all went to a storage place high above our clothes at the ranch.

Our son, who began hunting with his grandfather's shotgun, now shoots birds with his own shotgun which he leaves at the ranch where his two sons keep their toy guns in a drawer. In one of those inexplicable repetitions of family history, just as my grandmother did, their mother—though she too grew up with a hunting father—doesn't allow guns in their house in town. But she knows, as we all do, that even the most peace-loving boy will often imagine that the stick he picks up in the yard can be a sword or a gun. Like my father's dogs, the boys' plastic and wooden guns as well as their toy pistols have their place—outside in the country.

Our oldest grandson, twelve now, was allowed to use his father's rifle and to sit by his grandfather in a deer blind this season. He didn't get a shot but by shaking a pair of antlers together, he "rattled up" a buck, a primitive method, which for hunters answers a primitive need.

Under Guard

At the Giza Pyramids the first photo we took was of a black uniformed security guard wearing a black beret sitting on a camel, an AK-47 propped against his thigh. Others in the same uniform, also mounted on camels—chosen to compliment the site, I supposed—made a vast circle around the three pyramids. This small army was by no means the first one to reach the pyramids. Napoleon was once there and his troops, it has been long rumored, had used the nose of the guardian Sphinx for target practice. Napoleon, like Alexander, like Julius Caesar, like many another conqueror, was always being blamed for something. Those who refuse to assign blame even though it makes a good story, say that the desert sands and winds have eroded the nose of the Sphinx.

I waited in front of the Great Pyramid, my hair all plastered to one side of my face by a rising sandstorm. In spite of the sand stinging my face, I resisted the impulse to enter the tomb just to get out of the wind. So many buses had lined up carrying so many people, a wavering thread of them headed toward the gaping rocky entrance; the air would be bad inside. We climbed to the entrance anyway. On this first trip to Egypt, even with doubts about entering close, dark places, I was still eager to try everything. Light tubes covered by heavy plastic snaked along both sides of the narrow interior path. Thousands had been there before us, thousands had stooped as I was stooping, breathing stale air, bent almost double, through the space just big enough for a small sarcophagus. Short ladders along the way, their steps difficult to see in the dim light, demanded climbing. Like the people immediately in front of me and immediately behind—ladders somehow make closeness more obvious—I climbed, but I had already lost the little curiosity I had about the pyramid's interior.

Straightening up at last, I was relieved to see air holes, to see the sky. Toward the back stood the lidless black granite sarcophagus where the mummy of a pharaoh, Khufu, known as Cheops in Greek, once lay. Too large for the passage we'd followed, it might have been brought in by another passage or lowered from the pyramid's top. Unforgiving black granite walls surrounded us. Nothing else. One of the men in the group, the tall one dressed in white, patted the stone blocks composing each wall as if he were a prisoner searching for rock seams. What more was he hoping to find? His eagerness to discover what had already been discovered was somehow irritating. We were all walking a well-trodden path. No matter how we might try to recreate an initial explorer's fear and wonder, or even an early tomb robber's greed, we remained tourists who could explore only our own reactions. Mine was to get out of there. I wheeled around so quickly I brushed against a stranger in my hurry to the exit tunnel, the same one serving as an entrance. The return trip over the same trail, as usual, seemed shorter than the way we'd taken inside. Outside the sandy air stung my face again. I held onto the remnants of an old straw gardening hat I'd brought to guard against the Egyptian sun. Already dried by Texas sun, the wind had cracked its crown off the brim the first few minutes after I'd gotten off the bus. Later I bought a sand-colored scarf large enough to wrap round my head and tie round my neck, a western version of the *hijab* worn by so many of the young women I'd seen in Cairo although the *hijab* covers the shoulders as well. Even later I would buy one of those short-brimmed white canvas buckets that clutch the head, what the English call "a proper hat."

"You okay?" my husband asked.

I shook my head. It was early March, not quite yet the season called *Khamsin*, usually in late March and April, when sporadic sand storms were to be expected, nor had I expected to react so strongly against the interior trip through the Great Pyramid though its monumental architecture had been, from the first, overwhelming

Built somewhere around 2500 BC, the only one of the seven wonders of the ancient world still standing, it was indeed stunning. Imaginative pictures are mainly what's left of the other six: the temple of Artemis at Ephesus, the statue of Zeus at Olympia, the lighthouse at Alexandria, the mausoleum of Helicarnassus, the hanging gardens of Babylon, and the colossus of Rhodes. Usually the Great Pyramid is spoken of in terms of measurement. All I could see was a monument to eternity, although I knew ancient Egyptian pharaohs, at that time, believed in a reunion with the sun god. His pyramid's height put Khufu closer. Having ventured inside, I wanted to shake off the weight of centuries; there was no denying that heaviness, apparent as the reason for the black-clad guard with his gun. He was there for our protection, and his post near the bus parking lot may have been a prize one, for like every Egyptian whose picture we took, we gave him *bakseesh*. Although he kept our coins, he was the only one who did not ask for money. Was it beneath his dignity, or was it against his orders? We didn't really mind giving what little we did. Giving *bakseesh* partially absorbed our guilt about being Americans fortunate enough to travel in other countries.

—◆—

At first I thought the man wearing a suit sitting directly behind the driver might be his relief. On a tour where there were two of everything—an American lecturer and an Egyptian guide for tombs and temples, an American manager and his Egyptian counterpart—I thought there could be two bus drivers. After going to the Giza Pyramids and Khufu's reconstructed boat, the ceremonial one buried in pieces beside his tomb, after visiting the Sphinx and taking the obligatory pictures there, I realized the fellow behind the driver generally stayed on the bus. He was our plainclothes man. We all knew tourists had been shot in Egypt. But exactly when and where? Never good at remembering exact numbers, questions swirled through my head. Where were those people from? How many were Americans? If we were hated previously, weren't we more hated now since the war began in Iraq? In our desire to finally see Egypt, we'd put these thoughts in the backs of our minds. The care we were being given roused them again.

We also had four men wearing black berets and black uniforms with white leather belts, a few also wearing white diagonal shoulder straps vaguely reminiscent of the old Sam Browne belts once worn by British army officers. In an unmarked black car behind the bus, they followed us everywhere. The man sitting in front of the bus with the cell phone was on the lookout for terrorists in front, we said.

"He can warn the uniforms in back in case he spots the terrorists ahead," someone added. Gallows humor must be rampant among American tourists in the Mid-East. By exaggerating fear, perhaps we unconsciously hoped to brush aside our personal ones. However, I expected that most of us had already brushed our fears away as far as possible when we decided to go on the trip. Actually the one we'd planned to take in 2002 had been cancelled after the September 11, 2001 tragedy. In 2005, three years later, continually warned against going to Egypt by friends and family, we'd reassured everyone, "They wouldn't take us if it wasn't safe."

Now I found a plainclothes man, two guides, two managers, and a driver were herding us. Counting the men in the unmarked car, I realized there were ten herders to seventeen sheep, a ratio of one-point-seven travelers for every protector. Trying to forget the ridiculous number, I began counting something else. Five minarets appeared while riding through Cairo's outskirts. When it took us almost ten minutes to drive by part of the City of the Dead—Cairo's huge cemetery where the living poor occupied the crypts of the dead—I had to let the minarets fade. It would have been interesting to at least walk through part of that city, to see how people there survived, but that wasn't on the tour's program. We were traveling in Egypt like a group of cosseted Victorians only faster, and the Victorians usually carried their own teapots with them. Actually we had less contact with Egyptians than some Victorian tourists who had to wrangle meals, look after large trunks, hire guides, and make every kind of arrangement, most of which must have involved constant haggling.

The security guards in the unmarked black car never spoke to anyone on the tour. They didn't nod, hardly flicked an eyelid in our direction. Though we didn't refer to them often, everyone knew they were there. The black uniforms and the armed man in the suit were so omnipresent everyone quit paying much attention to them. In this way they gradually became as invisible as parents watching over children in an amusement park.

Seeing the worn white leather belts, badly fitting uniforms, and infinite boredom of the four men in the car, we were sorry they had to endure so many empty hours. At least the plainclothes man on the bus had the driver to talk to and sometimes he had someone on the other end of his cell phone. If, when climbing on the bus, anyone nodded at him, he nodded back. Whenever we stopped, the black car's doors were opened. Cigarette smoke writhed in the air, but the four men in the car hardly talked to each other. From their radio a static-scratched voice coughed out something in Arabic resembling the usual coded announcements heard in taxicabs. They didn't appear to be listening to it. I could have easily been wrong; maybe they attended to every word, or maybe the babble we heard on the radio was mere recitation of other cars' locations or a repetition of orders given to others. Whatever it was, it probably didn't pertain to us, and that was the problem; we seemed to be moving around the city in a big bubble.

If there was a place we could have been shot easily, it was within the enormous three-dimensional outline of a pyramid framing the Tomb of the Unknown Soldier and the Tomb of Anwar Sadat, where all seventeen of us were backlit by the setting sun. Many years after Sadat's assassination I heard his widow speak at a Planned Parenthood fundraiser and was impressed by her intelligence and her fiercely contained grief. Now before Sadat's highly polished black granite tomb four uniformed guards standing at attention apparently took turns standing at ease. In their red fezzes, tight-fitting red jackets, wide white sashes and baggy blue trousers, holding swords with blades pointing skyward more or less left, they resembled soldiers from some forgotten musical comedy. In front of the Unknown Soldier's Tomb stood two men wearing flimsy sateen shirts and trousers, cardboard-looking headdresses and wide cardboard-looking necklaces painted to resemble the ones found on royal mummies, equally fake arm bands and sashes with buckles of counterfeit gold. Each clung awkwardly to an extremely tall spear in his right hand. It was hard to feel any kind of awe even if the sun's dying light might have created a reverential mood. The others, busy snapping photos, were trying to take advantage of the last light while I waited to one side of the costumed guards feeling vaguely embarrassed for them. The people in charge of representative splendor had gotten it all wrong; it was bad theatre.

"Move on." My husband whispered behind me.

"Why?"

"You ought to know," he teased. "We're perfect silhouettes. Someone should call the security guards. They're all out of the car, sitting at the curb by the bus waiting for something to happen."

"You've always told me if someone wants to shoot us, they'll shoot us."

"Yes."

At that moment I felt a strange bravado. "I've decided not to worry. All these other people are worrying for us."

Despite our guards' sometimes brooding, sometimes half-forgetful vigilance, neither the bus nor a single person on the tour was attacked in Cairo.

Travel in Middle Egypt was off limits to us due to a series of attacks on tourists and other foreigners by militant Islamic fundamentalists in 1992. No one in our group remembered any of those incidents thirteen years later. Some recalled the shootings at Luxor mainly, I think, only because of the proximity of the site and their vague memories of the large number of victims. We flew over Middle Egypt, from Cairo to Luxor, one night, leaving our plainclothes man and four followers in black behind.

At the airport I was selected for the more rigorous search. Arms and legs had to be stretched as in Da Vinci's famous drawing showing the ideal proportions of the human body. Now our protectors turned into accusers, one of those strange role switches taking place all over the world, one so familiar it was hard to remember a time when plane passengers weren't subject to search.

Egypt Air was an hour late. Nobody cared. We were too exhausted. Energy we might have spent complaining had to be saved for the next day.

Standing in front of the Luxor temple the following morning, half-listening to our Egyptian guide, I wondered aloud if this was the place where the tourists had been shot.

Seven or eight others on the tour stared at me either directly, or like one woman from San Francisco, gave me a sideways glance as if she were saying, "Oh, why bring that up!"

The oldest man on the tour whispered, "In ninety-seven wasn't it?"

"Not here," the American guide said. "It didn't happen here."

"So where?"

"Hatshepsut's temple. We'll see it tomorrow."

Our Egyptian guide broke in then to explain the carvings on the temple's facade. Like every site, Luxor it had its share of uniformed guards, but unlike the places we had visited before, it was so crowded that the guide had to speak via a microphone attached by a band to his head. By broadcasting his voice, he could reach each one of us also wearing headsets looped over our heads. Private amplifiers wired to something resembling a black plastic question mark hung from every ear in the group. Technology wins, I decided while sitting on one of many stones polished by innumerable other bottoms that had landed there before. It was cold. The vastness of thousands of years of human history yawned behind me. I would have liked another cup of tea, but there wasn't time for it that morning. In Egypt where recorded centuries were towering piles, there was never time enough on tour for ordinary life, but traveling on our own wasn't a real choice for us in Egypt after 9/11.

Hatshepsut's temple at Deir El-Bahri near Luxor suited what little we really knew of her; she served as regent for her young nephew Tuthmosis III for seven years, assumed the title and ceremonial beard of pharaoh, and ruled as his co-regent for fifteen more years. Vast as any of the other royal funerary temples, her place had a commanding rock cliff behind it. Three tiers of colonnades rose from terraces approached by giant ramps, probably used by religious processions as well as by today's tourists. One of the few queens to become a pharaoh, she left her own colossal stone tribute to uppity women. On the second terrace the usual black uniformed guard with an AK-47 was on duty next to a plaque commemorating the deaths of fifty-eight foreigners and four Egyptians gunned down by Islamic terrorists on November 17, 1997. Later I learned that none of the dead were Americans. Stunned by heat and light reflected by white limestone, I read the plaque before moving inside to be surrounded by the crowd of Italians, Japanese, French, Germans, and a few English. I saw no other Americans at Hatshepsut's temple that morning. We came across only one other small group of our countrymen seeing ancient sites during our two weeks in Egypt. Others may have been there but not in great numbers.

As we left Hatshepsut's temple, a strong wind rose and I decided it was time to buy the "proper hat" from one of the many bazaars lining the road to the parking lot. Here the required ritual of bargaining nearly made us miss the bus. No one wants to make that much of a nuisance of oneself, no one wants to be the laggard that holds up everyone else, no one wants to be left behind. By that time, in that place, the idea of being abandoned, no matter how foolish, seemed more terrible than being shot.

Terrorized by my own imagination, I shouted, "Don't wait for the change," and grabbed the hat. My husband grabbed my hand and we ran to meet the manager who was looking for us. My anti-tour feelings began to fade as the wind obscured our footprints leading to the bus.

That afternoon we went on to the Valley of the Kings with its buried *folies de granduer* —all the tombs had been looted, even Tutankhamun's. But robbers there were apparently frightened away early, many years before Howard Carter discovered its riches nearly intact in 1922. Because of the number of visitors, our guides had to decide quickly which tomb could hold us all. Every group seemed to be in danger of being in the same place at once. When we returned to the Temple of Luxor to view its well-lit splendor that night, our Egyptian guide, taking in the tremendous crowd, exclaimed, "This is crazy!"

The following day, I asked our American manager, "Is traveling here always like this?"

He shook his head. "Security wants us all in one place. We're easier to guard that way."

They were back—I finally noticed—the black uniformed men all around the docks had become so ubiquitous I hadn't seen them.

When we'd boarded the riverboat in Luxor, we could give ourselves over to gilded dreams of the past. Looking out the long half-windowed wall of our stateroom, we could imagine we'd boarded Khufu's marvelous barge and were going to be rowed up the Nile to take part in a yearly festival. But by the time we'd sailed as far south as Kom Ombo, the site of a double temple near Aswan, the crowd had assembled again. Thirty-eight Nile riverboats full of passengers were maneuvering toward the dock. Just as a plane does over an over-crowded landing strip, we circled. Today's Nile boats—in contrast to the opulent steamer moving alone down the river in the film version of *Death on the Nile*—are four-storied floating hotels; beside staterooms, there are separate dining rooms, lounges that double as night clubs with a dance floor and bar, and sundecks including, on some, minuscule swimming pools. To pilot thirty-eight of these hotels around each other took considerable skill. We stood on our boat's sundeck and waved to the other tourists we were passing so close to on their sundecks. Finally our pilot was able to dock by "sandwiching" his boat between two others. In order to get to the temple, one had to walk through the lobbies of one or two other boats, depending on whether you were bread or filling. Seeing the crowd on shore, I could be neither. I already had tomb fatigue; now temple fatigue set in. Viewing the temple at Kom Obo from the sundeck, the setting sun made me into another perfect silhouette, something I realized much later. Travelers have a particular forgetfulness about the continual possibility of danger. Entranced by novelty, we were too much in the world. For me lack of awareness, in the midst of so many ancient Egyptian tombs, had become a willful desire.

While at Aswan one morning when it was too windy for feluccas, we boarded small launches and crossed the Nile for a twenty-minute camel ride to reach the monastery of St. Simeon. Here again, we were perfect targets strung out in a wavering line on the desert, everyone walking or riding camels led by their Egyptian drivers. The security guards, if there were any, were out of sight. It was a cool bright day, a brief time to revel in the desert's vast sweep, the richly varying colors of the sand, the sudden appearance of other camel riders moving swiftly across a dune in the distance. We were too distracted trying to learn how to accommodate our bodies to a camel's swaying gait to be concerned about silhouettes. Camels are harder to ride than horses, a lot noisier, and by temperament, protestors. When we first mounted, snorts and groans rose as they lurched from a sitting position with all four legs neatly tucked under to poke two front feet in the sand followed by an equal lurch as their two rear knees unfolded. It was like being thrown forward then back in a monster rocking chair. Clinging to the wooden saddle pommel, I felt whoever designed a saddle for this absurdly elegant creature with a hump on its back had to be an ingenious as well as a needy rider.

At both hotels in Cairo we stayed in, one going and one returning, there was a guard on every floor, usually in the hall outside the elevators. In Aswan at the Old Cataract Hotel, none were evident though the waiter who brought us drinks at sunset could have been a plainclothes man, or maybe the apparently ordinary men loitering around the edge of the verandah overlooking the Nile were really looking for approaching terrorists. After ten days in Egypt, I'd begun staring hard at people who were probably totally innocent of guard duty.

On the following day after getting up at 5:00 A.M. to catch a plane to Abu Simbel, I discovered another good reason to be thankful for protectors. A stomach virus making some of the others ill hit me as I stepped off the bus at the Aswan airport.

"Oh, I'm sick." I said, barely missing vomiting on our American manager's feet. It wasn't one of those once-you-throw-up-you're-over-it sicknesses. It kept on. I just missed the airport's marble floor by finding a trash can instead, then in front of five early morning janitors—shouting something in Arabic—I made a great splash on the floor just outside the locked Women's Room door. The janitors kept pointing to the left. I followed their signals down the marble-covered hall to an open Women's Room.

After a flurry of apologies on my part, fast decisions, and hurried preparations, I was driven back to the boat accompanied by a new guide from Aswan who spoke English and kept reassuring me that the tour would return from Abu Simbel and pick me up. At the boat I was given a dark, quiet room with an adjoining bath. There I lay sleeping fitfully like the "lady of high degree" having "chills and fever, fever and chills," thinking of those undaunted nineteenth century English women travelers like Isabel Burton and Jane Digby. Did they ever get sick? In a few hours the phone rang and a calm voice announced the car was there to take me back to the airport.

In those few hours my husband, along with everyone else on our tour, had flown to Abu Simbel and back. Temple fatigued as I was, I wished I could have seen the site saved from Lake Nasser when the new high dam was built. When it came to most famous locations, I was as compulsive a tourist as anyone; it didn't matter how many times I'd seen pictures, painted or photographed, I wanted to see the place, though I would have preferred to have seen it as my friend, a cultural anthropologist, did. He sailed up the Nile in a felucca before the new dam was built and spent the night sleeping on a sandbar at the monumental feet of Ramses II, where he vowed fighting sand flies took the romance out of the whole adventure.

Air Egypt, an hour late as usual, took us back to Cairo from Aswan in time to make another trip with everyone to the dusty, cluttered Cairo Museum before we flew home. Some of King Tut's tomb treasures, we were told, were on tour in the U.S. There were many rooms full of royal jewels, sarcophagi, gilded furniture and chariots, armies of miniature pottery armies. Only by noticing discrete signs now and then could we tell anything was missing. No one was allowed to take pictures in the museum. The last picture we took was of a young guard wearing army camouflage standing outside the Cairo Museum in the shade, his AK-47 slung over his shoulder.

Like most travelers, after we returned I continued to be interested in the country most recently visited, though I focused on the fate of tourists in Egypt. In April 2005, seven were wounded in one of Cairo's downtown squares, and a woman who shot at a tourist bus killed her accomplice and herself but no one else. Then in July came the massive attacks at the Egyptian Red Sea resort, Sharm El-Sheik. Eighty-eight were confirmed dead. These tourists were all in one place, all sleeping in one town just as we had been on the Nile except our boats were anchored two and three deep by the docks while the vacationers at Sharm El-Sheik slept on land. Perhaps we were simply lucky, or perhaps because of the effect on Nile tourism after the slaughter at Hatshepsut's temple in 1997, we were, ironically, more closely guarded. And if we were, the greater irony is that since so much international tourist money is spent on the trip up the Nile, that valuable river remains the more valuable site, a point of view I find neither comfortable nor necessarily true. Those tourists at Sharm El-Sheik were chosen as targets just as were those at Hatshepsut's temple, I believe, by accident compounded by old, unknown, perhaps unknowable, grudges. Most of us are innocents abroad; we may stumble into accident by traveling toward one. We are only more conscious of threat when we're in another country and always under guard.

Now, in February 2011, six years later with Egypt in turmoil, I look back at that trip with its constant tense undercurrents. No one spoke kindly of Mubarak even then. The novel, *The Yacoubian Building*, by Alaa-Al-Aswany, first published in Arabic in 2002, was translated into English in 2004. Reading it after returning from Egypt, I found an array of people including a newspaper editor, a millionaire, an elderly roué, a worker, a young girl, and other parts of a society interacting in a country ridden with corruption and repression. The most impoverished character's innocent enlistment in a militant group of terrorists, which leads to his death as a martyr, is symbolic of the eventually unbearable frustrations prevailing.

Watching Tahrir Square filled with televised crowds vehemently protesting, sometimes defending themselves from government-provided, camel-mounted men snapping long whips, an old form of subjugation and a reminder of slavery, to meet even older, more primitive rock-throwing attacks, we could witness the Egyptians' elemental rage. And a wild joy over the freedom to express it. At this point however, I can only wish for resolutions that will once more allow contemporary Egyptians to wander safely through every square and unguarded tourists to wander as well through Egypt's ancient civilizations.

The Galapagos

A Booby Tour

We got up at 4:00 a.m. to drive to the Austin airport in time to meet the two-hours-before-an-international-flight demand, one of those horrid rules the airlines make. "They need to check and scan baggage," our travel agent told us. "It's the set-up for the entire trip." They wouldn't have found anything unusual except perhaps an excess of sunscreen. We were on our way to the Gala-pagos via Dallas, a forty-five minute flight. The next plane to Miami, a three-hour flight, left an hour late leaving us imprisoned in our seats and resulting in one of those breath-taking trots to the flight from Miami to Quito where we landed, still in our own central stan-dard time zone but two hours from town because a new airport was being built at that distance. We reached the capitol by 8:00 p.m. approximately fourteen hours after we began this self-inflicted travail.

It's a widely held belief that travelers, like women in childbirth, forget the pain after the baby is born, or the trip is over. In my case, neither is true. And we weren't even finished. After three days in Quito, another 4:00 a.m. leave-taking took us to Guayaquil, then two hours from there we were on the landing strip at Baltra Island, a flat speck of ground next to the steamy island of Santa Cruz—85° F and humid as were all the islands we visited. There are thirteen major volcanic islands and six minor ones approximately 600 miles off the west coast of Ecuador, too many to visit in a week, so we chose a western itinerary including Isabela, Fernandina, Santiago, and others plus a great number of bays. (The UNESCO website says 127 islands exist in the Galapagos, but their official count includes islets and large rocks.)

Mauricio, our naturalist guide, led us to a bus, which took us across Baltra to a ferry crossing the channel between Baltra and Santa Cruz. After landing on Santa Cruz, we climbed on another bus to an inland lunch at a private ecological reserve where we saw our first giant tortoises—enormous, gray-black creatures sitting in mud baths—then to the bus again, crawling across the island stopping only for our first nature walk to see two collapsed green-filled craters before finally arriving at Puerto Ayora. We walked carefully around several sea lions asleep on the dock before boarding a dinghy, the inflated rubber-like type with an outboard motor attached called a "panga" in this part of the world. The panga carried us across a bay to a ladder dangling off the side of a small swaying wooden platform and another ladder leading to the boat's deck. Climbing up the various ladders using help from the arms and hands of strong crewmen in the panga and two more sailors swaying in the platform above, I became a clumsy monkey. When finally on deck—I have no idea how many hours it took us to arrive after our 4:00 a.m. rising in Quito—

I decided I was too old for this trip, one I'd insisted on taking. Why, at almost seventy-nine, had I talked my eighty-one-year-old husband into this? We attempted to keep in shape by walking briskly approximately three miles for forty-five minutes, four days a week, but was that sufficient? Our daughter, Claire, who belonged to a gym and swam regularly, was the fittest of the three of us. It soon became evident after the rest of the group scrambled up the ladders—they too had to have help— my husband and I were, by far, the oldest passengers aboard. What did I hope to accomplish by putting us in harm's way on a sixteen-passenger motorized-sailing ship in the Pacific Ocean for eight days and seven nights? Why had I insisted on this journey? I knew, in part, why my husband had; he loved the looks of the ship, a barkentine with over ten thousand square feet of canvas, enough to satisfy a man who'd read all of Patrick O'Brien's sailing novels set during England's Napoleonic wars. And I was equally attracted by the sheer beauty of the ship even though previous passengers told us the sails weren't used often.

Curiosity, that great provoker, is another answer. I'd started reading Darwin's *Voyage of the Beagle*. The scientific terms were, at first, overwhelming to one not versed in Latin or to any of the disciplines such as entomology and botany Darwin knew well. An undergraduate course in geology, however, was helpful. Generally I glided through the terms and got on with his recollections of his voyage beginning in 1831 when he was twenty-six. First published in 1839 and revised by Darwin in 1845, they are charming as well as adventurous. During his five years away from England, he spent a little more than three on land, and in that time, months on horseback often dodging native Indians warring with encroaching Argentinians as well as wending his way through a revolution.

The other source of my wish to go to the Galapagos was an *Austin-Statesman* newspaper photograph of a Blue-footed Booby perched on the diving board of a swimming pool near Lake Travis, part of the chain of lakes made by damming the Colorado River. The Booby, quite alone, looked a little foolish, as the name, derived from the Spanish word "bobo" meaning fool or clown, implies. Nevertheless, having missed one near Austin, I longed to see this particular Booby. There are different kinds, including a Red-footed Booby, although I didn't find it nearly as intriguing. I'm not a birder so I will admit whim, that small action that changes everything, partially governed my choice to visit the islands. I also admit a predilection for exotic names. Perhaps it was the same urge that used to take other travelers to Timbuktu or Bora Bora.

One of Wikipedia's writers says, "The Blue-footed Booby was first studied extensively by Charles Darwin during his trip to the Galapagos Islands." However our guide, who studied at the Charles Darwin Center, said, "The Boobies were not in the Galapagos when Darwin visited. Probably they migrated from Peru later."

Whose word to trust? I took Mauricio's. "Darwin studied the finches," he insisted. Small dark brown birds, the finches are rather ordinary looking. We knew Darwin noted some of the their beaks had grown larger in order to take advantage of the best food supply: "...one might really fancy that from an original paucity of birds in this archipelago, one species had been taken and modified for different ends." Here is one of those startling statements where the seeds of Darwin's later theory of evolution via natural selection can be found. A reader keeps asking silently, "Don't you see? It's evolution!" This foreknowledge of his eventual realization pushes one on via an after-the-fact collaboration with the formation of an idea.

When we first saw a Booby involved in a courting ritual lifting his feet one-by-one I was struck by his resemblance to the giant-shod circus clowns of my childhood. In order to walk, they had first to flap their huge shoes up. The male Booby's intention, however, is different; he is lifting his feet to show them off to a female who is mainly interested in mating a fellow with the most beautiful blue feet. Generally, Mauricio told us, she prefers the lighter, brighter, almost neon colored ones, of the younger males.

Another courting ritual is reminiscent of the male peacock's. Rather than the colorful display of fanned-out feathers, the male Booby unfurls both brownish wings and points his long beak toward the sky while raising his tail. What this "sky pointing" proves is, as far as I can discover, unknown. A good deal of noisy intermittent beak clacking and beak rubbing on each other's necks progresses. Blue-footed Boobies mate for life, said Mauricio, but they must reenact the courtship ritual every year, "like an anniversary," he commented. "Like a renewal of vows," said another traveler who succumbed, as many of us do, to anthropomorphizing. We are Boobies in our own way: since our willingness to anthropomorphize is almost impossible to overcome, we are apparently stuck with the egocentricity of the human race.

The first sight we had of courtship rituals was after landing on a beach where we were able to look up to a pair on a small dirt ledge, rather like looking up to a marionette show, to see them perform. They are large, white-breasted birds with long brown-gray wings. Their necks and heads are brown and white, and their yellow eyes stare from either side of their long pointed bills. Males, we were told, have more yellow in their irises. Females are usually larger, but I found sizes and eye colors difficult to differentiate since my own eyes were drawn to their duck-like webbed feet, light turquoise to dark aqua. I can't say if a darker blue indicates age. Getting into unknowns such as this, I realized again my scientific limitations. Boobies were rather endearing looking, but the necessity of parent boobies' disgusting practice of allowing the first and largest chick to kill his/her sibling at times when food was scarce had to be admitted. This is done quite literally; the largest chick pushes the smallest one out of the nest while their mother stares into the distance, not a scene we had to witness, but one shown on a Netflix film viewed after returning. Objectivity can be hard to come by when the apparently endearing turns savage. But long ago most of us learned Tennyson's phrase, "nature red in tooth and claw," always useful and so superior sounding. All too often, unfortunately, it sometimes describes human nature as well.

On other islands we found more Boobies flashing their feet, easily seen against the black volcanic rock. Like all the wildlife in the Galapagos, they were unafraid of humans. Sometimes we were close enough to touch them although we'd been warned not to. We could take all the pictures we wanted, but we were never to even consider petting a sea lion, a yellow-orange land or black marine iguana—with their miniature dragon-scaly backs they weren't hard to resist. All the fur seals were too far away, as were the flamingos, the little penguins we saw chose precarious rocks, and we wouldn't have dared to interrupt frigate birds puffing out great red balloons from their throat pouches trying to attract females.

Visitors used to try to ride the giant tortoises. Darwin wrote, "I frequently got on their {tortoises} backs and then giving a few raps on the hinder part of their shells, they would rise up and walk away; but I found it very difficult to keep my balance." In whaling days, the tortoises were taken aboard ship as a long-lived fresh meat supply. Since the tortoises were almost decimated and a breeding program had to be started, touching one was déclassé. However if an animal or bird on land or in the ocean happened to be near us, it was perfectly all right for them to come closer.

While snorkeling my husband felt a sea lion's ripple across his back; other visitors told of swimming with manta rays. The very idea of being near a ray's wide wings gave me the shudders. I remembered too well a mantra ray stinging a friend on his ankle while he waded the shallow sands of the Gulf of Mexico. He spent the next two weeks in a hospital's ward recovering from surgery. The rays' lovely dark wing patterns seen from above while drifting in a panga were as close as I'll ever want to get. Claire, our daughter who has snorkeled in the Antilles area, off the Pacific coast of Mexico, and in the U.S. Virgin Islands, felt a sea turtle gliding by underneath her; marine iguanas dove just past to feed on the algae, and a cormorant whizzed by on his deep sea dive for food. So, while birds and animals didn't actually touch us, sometimes we'd feel beady eyes upon us or a sea lion flopped nearer to stare. The Galapagos are the dominion of the wildlife and have been even before Darwin's day. Except for tortoise grabbing, none of the animals or birds have been hunted. Now they're all protected in the Ecuador National Park area, which is ninety-seven per cent of the Galapagos land surface, and since 1979 has also been a UNESCO World Heritage Site. According to UNESCO, the site accommodates 30,000 inhabitants and 170,000 tourists each year. Scheduling was so well organized we didn't see another group on the same island but once, and their guide quickly set them on another route.

While we were visiting, our usual schedule was: 6:30 a.m. rising followed by breakfast on the deck. By 8:00 a.m. we've gotten on life jackets, boarded the pangas, and around 8:30 a.m. we've made a wet landing by wading the last few yards or a dry landing on one of the islands where we're given an hour or more hiking tour while Mauricio told us what we're seeing followed by swimming or snorkeling or perhaps a panga ride to see unusual vegetation and whatever fish or birds were available, then we returned to the ship for lunch. An hour after lunch we were usually at another island where we followed a variation of the morning's trip, which might include kayaking, a visit to a town, or a longer snorkel time. Supper was at 6:30 p.m. We all ate like starving sharks and were abed in our air-conditioned cabins by 9:30 p.m.

The second day of our voyage while snorkeling toward two large black rocks where we were told we could see a number of colorful fish, my husband, in trouble with a leaky face mask, felt something tugging on his life jacket, and looked up long enough to see our guide pulling him along. I wished Mauricio was with me when I was falling off the panga backward, the only way to go when wearing flippers, and realized there was no beach in sight. My only experience of ocean swimming was in the warm waters of the Gulf of Mexico, off the gently sloping beaches of Galveston Island, and in the equally warm waters of the Mexican Caribbean off Cozumel. Although we'd chosen to go to the Galapagos in early April before the cold Humboldt Current arrived, the water I fell into was remarkably cool, there was no welcoming beach anywhere, and like the majority of the group, I hadn't put on a life jacket. I felt like a child who'd just noticed her mother had vanished.

Instead, those two large black rocks stood alone in the distance where everyone else headed. The first time I looked down I could see nothing but a hundred or more little gray sharks through my leaking mask, so naturally I swam toward the group, or I thought I did. It took only a minute to realize I was caught by a current, one Mauricio had warned us about, pulling me in a distinctly different direction away from the black rocks. I'd never looked upon them favorably. They were only glistening black lumps that colorful fish liked. As we'd been told to do, I raised one arm and a panga arrived to pluck me from the ocean, another one those easier-said-than-done instances. How does one walk up a dangling rope ladder's rounded wooden rings with flippers on in a pushy, current-filled sea? First I tried foolishly to hook a flipper though a ladder's rung. I got one to go through, but this left me splayed out like a giant frog while the free flipper on my other foot idly flopped around. It had to come off and it had to be done with one hand. This was one of those instant-learning necessities I comprehended while the panga's pilot shouted at me to do the same thing my body had just understood.

"Yes! Yes," I shouted back trying to pull the obdurate piece of plastic off my foot.

The English fellow-passenger, a woman who was usually sketching an animal while the rest of us gaped at it, was the only other person on the panga, and her duty at the time was to rest all her weight on the reverse side of the boat while the pilot kept one hand on the outboard motor and the other stretched toward me, struggling with the ladder, the flippers, and the constantly rocking sea. I finally disentangled myself and slid over the fat rim of the panga to wrap up in a blue towel and sit opposite the English woman. Why was she there? She'd mentioned she was a diver who had completed seventy-five deep-sea dives—I'm genuinely interested in others' exploits, particularly when they're numbered—and scorned snorkeling. Perhaps she only came along for the ride; perhaps she wanted to see whatever she could. I remember how artist friends react to any sort of action; they are terribly fond of seeing.

The English woman tossed another towel to me and warned, "Don't catch cold," one of those utterly useless well meant admonitions our common language provides. Nevertheless her accent gives me a comforting vision of teapots, their hot spouts steaming in the air surrounding us. Then a strong selfish wish arose: I wanted everyone else to give up staring at fish in the ocean surrounding the wretched rocks and swim immediately to the two pangas so we might return to the ship anchored a comfortable distance behind us. But they were all worse than the artist about seeing; they were still entranced by the fish below the surface. I spent thirty minutes more swathed in towels waiting, watching them bob bottom-side-up around the rocks resigning myself to the pleasures of others while knowing I never need to attempt swimming in an open sea again.

Immediately after getting back on the ship I came down with a definite allergic reaction to—What could it be? I'd been inoculated against every pollen existing in Austin, a place marked in black on allergy maps. I am, in fact, one of my allergist's star examples of the extraordinary freedom shots and drops can provide, but the Galapagos, stuck in the equatorial realms of the Pacific, are another part of the world. Something there made me sneeze, made my eyes water, gave me a runny nose; all combined in a too-familiar first day of a bad cold reaction. The trouble was every day continued like the first day no matter how much of my own plus my daughter's antihistamines and nose drops I took.

Despite my great curiosity about the next islands, the different white, olivine, and black beaches, the rare fish Mauricio promised awaited swimmers and snorkelers, I knew I couldn't see them with a runny nose. I could do nothing but lay about on the deck on top of comfortably plump royal blue seats on the banquettes surrounding our dining tables. Under an equally blue tarp rigged to protect passengers from too much sun, I snuffled through the remainder of Darwin's *Voyage of the Beagle*. Without anyone else's schedule pending, I had at last an unplanned vacation, and every day my husband and daughter brought me more photographs they'd taken of Blue-footed Boobies.

Mingling With the Scots

Eleven years after WW II was over, in October 1956, we arrived in the middle of a village in the Scottish Highlands in the middle of the day carrying our luggage and expecting to find a room in the first hotel we happened upon. We soon discovered there was only one in Arrochar, near what was once the McFarland clan's small territory between Loch Long and Loch Lomand. We'd been encouraged to go there by my husband's grandfather, John B. McFarland. Spelling variations are ongoing—MacFarlane, McFarlane, McFarlin, McFarlen, to select a few. My husband, Joe, wanted to see the country his mother's people were from, and even greater than a beloved grandfather's desire and our own curiosity, for I joined him in this, was our naiveté.

We did know something about the need for research. There were tombstones at former family farms near Morristown, in East Tennessee, dating back to the 1850s, Granddad's memories covered the years from the 1880s, *Ramsey's Annals of Tennessee* and county histories were available, and another McFarland volunteered a sketchy genealogy. But to our way of thinking, the best way to learn about a family's past was to go to the country where the family Bible and your elders said they were from. We hadn't the least idea what we were going to do once we arrived. Nevertheless we took our first leave from the U.S. Army of Occupation in Germany, flew to London, boarded a train to Edinburgh, and finally got on a Highland bus which wound for several hours through barren green-brown hills with trickles of water running down their sides.

Accustomed to the Sangre de Cristo branch of the Rocky Mountains in New Mexico, where the tallest peak, Wheeler, rises 13,160 feet, and the family vacation cabin near Tres Ritos is at approximately 8,000 ft., it was puzzling, at first, to understand why these Scottish hills had always been designated as "mountains." The highest, we'd read, was Ben Nevis at 4,406 feet. I thought about the early Scotch immigrants to the U.S., including some of the McFarlands who supposedly felt at home in the misty Appalachians though they were a good bit higher, Mount Mitchell in North Carolina is the highest at 6,684 feet. Of course, we decided it was useless to argue; if the natives said the Highlands were "mountains," these were mountains.

⸻ ⋈ ⸻

We'd already done enough searching to fill a small privately-printed book for the family about our branch of the McFarlands where we included a general history of the clan derived from Scribner's Sons, 10th edition of *The Scottish Clans and Their Tartans*. Much of our text consisted of letters from McFarland men fighting for the south during the Civil War. Joe had found them while venturing into his great-grandfather's Tennessee farmhouse attic one night, holding a kerosene lamp, and nearly stumbling over a chest full of rat-nibbled papers. There was nothing he'd rather have discovered, for among the ink-blotted letters scrawled in haste a young soldier's voice could be heard. Above all we wanted to preserve those letters written by this Confederate foot soldier with little schooling but great gifts of reliable reporting about what he was enduring. John Tate McFarland, 26, and six generations away from Scotland wrote his father in Morristown, Tennessee:

> State of Tenneese Roan Coynty
> Loudon June the 16 1861
> ...When we got to knoxville we wer al dry for water and no man was allowed to break ranks to get watter for there was no time loost. I seen a dime paid for a bucket of water and it was carried in a slop bucket....

On March 24, 1862 at a place called Iuka, Mississippi before the battle of Shiloh John Tate wrote:

> I cannot say that I am eager for a fight but it would be a pleasure to me to se the yankies well whipped one time before I come home. there is one thing about fighting we cant fight without some one getting killed....

After the battle of Shiloh, he reported:

April th 8 1862
Corinth Missippi
...the enemy was giving away though th boms wer flying and bursting in every direction the clashing of musketry was almost deafning. we got in sight of the enemy we fired a few rounds at them and then made at them with our bayonets...the yankies soon throghed down their guns....

Later in the same letter he recorded:

...we had to leave the battle field in possession of the enemy our regiment is badly cut to peaces. as to the number of ded I know nothing about the number. there is a great many thoug on both sides....

Wounded twice, John Tate McFarland, survived to marry a schoolteacher, move his bride to Texas, and become the father of our grandfather. After eleven years away from Tennessee, he wrote back, "to know anything about a country or a people you have to settle and cultivate the soil and mingle with the people."

Obviously we couldn't settle, nor could we become Scottish farmers, but we hoped to see more of the country and mingle with the people.

To get to certain areas, we hired a car and a driver, MacTavish—dark-haired, dark-eyed, of medium height, amiable, good humored, a native. Army service in the war must have wiped out much of his brogue, for we understood him readily. I never saw him in a kilt; he always wore a pair of old brown corduroys, a clean shirt, and a darker brown jacket. He was the one who introduced us to Miss Sheena McFarland, the only McFarland still living in Arrochar then. During earlier days, she worked on ships as a cruise director organizing activities for passengers. I suppose she contacted entertainers, planned dances, scheduled shuffleboard lessons, told people the best stores to visit when they landed, found fourths for bridge, stocked the library. Somehow she made a job out of other people's play. She was a small, sturdy, opinionated woman, sure of herself in the world.

"I've always said if you get lost somewhere just stand in the middle of a street, say your name, 'I'm Miss Sheena McFarland from Arrochar, Scotland,' slowly in good, clear English, announce you're lost, and ask for help."

I've never tried it, however I could easily see Miss Shenna in her sensible shoes standing the middle of a street, in some place like Singapore speaking good, clear English slowly, determined to be found. I thought her so fearless, so imperturbable that I was surprised to find a well-known plea worked in multi-colored embroidery, framed, and hung over her kitchen sink:

> From ghoulies and ghosties and
> Long leggety beasties
> And things that go bump in the night,
> Good Lord, deliver us.

She didn't seem to be the sort needing deliverance from anything.

We had read that Loch Sloy was the McFarland's ancestral gathering place in the hills surrounding Arrochar, so we wanted MacTavish to drive us up there. Unfortunately, a large hydroelectric plant that generated power from the lake plus a number of surrounding streams blocked our way. MacTavish insisted the only way we could see Loch Sloy was to tour the plant and feign interest in the production of electricity. How much of this was true and how much depended on MacTavish's need for paying passengers, we couldn't be sure. And mixed with that, I slowly understood, was his genuine pride in the plant. Our educations had provided us with a good background in the liberal arts, but gave us scant preparation for making intelligent comments on turbines.

My husband, born on a farm in the Panhandle of Texas, a part of the country that normally receives only eighteen inches of rainfall per year, could show genuine appreciation in the form of questions such as: "How far away is the loch?" And, "How much electricity does your plant produce?"

We wandered over the giant shining heaps of turbines on a catwalk that led us, eventually, back outside to MacTavish's black car and the road up to Loch Sloy, a disappointing sight, I felt, as it was only a small, slate-colored lake lightly rippling under gathering gray-white clouds, and surrounded by barren grayish-brown hills, the color of most the country above the tree line that time of year. Lower mountains wore the deep green, equally thin cover of various mosses, heather, and according to MacTavish, bracken. How could a McFarland clan member draw his broadsword and rush into battle crying, "Loch Sloy!" with any true sentiment about this mournful looking ancestral homeland? Love of country, I gathered, might be partially compelled by what one was accustomed to. Before moving to Texas, I had spent my early years in Middle Tennessee's hilly green and tree-covered country. Because the army had sent Joe to Pirmasens, we were assigned to officers' quarters in a former German *kaserne* in the western Rhineland Palatinate, I looked out our third story apartment windows every day at a lush, varicolored quilt of cultivated farmland where all my need of green was granted.

Loch Sloy appeared to be an undistinguished body of water although I'd seen its name on a picture in Joe's family's home blazoned on a red banner across a silver shield with the motto, "This I'll Defend" in a dark hallway. I don't think anyone paid much attention to the shield, for despite his grandfather's curiosity no one else in the family apparently wondered much about their forebears. As a former southerner, I thought my husband's family's disinterest was especially western. After all, my father-in-law had broken ground in plains soil that had never been farmed before. Like many others, although they had strong family bonds and land adjoining, their heads were turned toward the future. The picture of the shield in the hall, we decided, was probably a gift by a well-meaning friend who had ordered it by mail, in those pre-internet days, from any number of companies in the U.S. and Great Britain.

Similar ancient-looking pieces of heraldry to suit everybody are available now via the web; viewers without clan names are urged by one American company to concoct their own coats of arms and crests. You can choose among gyrfalcons, knights, eagles, lions, heads of armored knights, crossed swords, dragons, etc. One MacFarland version, and there are many—succeeding generations needed to distinguish theirs from the original—shows the chesty top half of a naked man called a "demi-savage" or "wild man," holding a sheaf of arrows, while on either side below a shield with a wavy crisscross and rosettes in each quarter, are two fully dressed, plaid-coated men in kilts wearing tams and knee-length plaid socks. "This I'll Defend" has become an allusion to a royal crown the demi-savage is pointing to with his left hand. Evidently a ruler sometimes awarded such coats of arms to a clan's chief for loyalty when his clan was on the ruler's winning side of a battle. I'm uncertain as to the heraldic meaning of a "demi-savage," but the term may refer to ferocity. Certainly, except for MacTavish and the two of us, there was no hint of any kind of humanity, half-wild or otherwise, around Loch Sloy that day.

We took pictures of the lake, climbed back in the car and returned to Arrochar just as a hard rain began.

"Worth a tour of the plant?" MacTavish asked.

"Oh, yes." We didn't want to let him down.

"Tomorrow we'll try for the Island Ivaugh—pronounced of-oo—and Inveruglas. I'll drive you over to Loch Lomand."

My spirits rose once more. We'd found we might be able to visit the two islands in Loch Lomand associated with the McFarlands by hiring a boat from one of the resorts on the shores of the lake.

Traveling on a second lieutenant's pay even when the exchange of dollars to British pounds was favorable, it would have been impossible to pay for a driver and to rent a boat for a half-day's outing. Extra funding from Grandfather McFarland, who wanted to know more of the "ancient history" of his family, gave us the luxury of extra expense.

From Arrochar beside the tidal Loch Long it was a quick trip east to Loch Lomond, the largest—twenty-four miles—fresh water lake in Great Britain. It was, we were told, five miles wide in some places. I knew part of the song, the chorus many know:

> You take the high road and I'll take the low road
> And I'll be in Scotland before you.
> For me and my true love will never meet again
> On the bonnie, bonnie banks of Loch Lomand.

I can't say where I first heard it; folk music seems to drift in the air and fall down through the generations long after the original meaning of the words is forgotten, though many others have wondered exactly who the "true love" was and why they will never meet again.

The touring boat, the Rob Roy, named after the Highland outlaw popularized by Sir Walter Scott, waited for us. Aboard we found two young English women, waitresses from a hotel bordering the lake, invited we supposed, by the captain.

We'd much preferred MacTavish's company, but he had to stay with his car. It was a large boat, and I had no real cause to complain until after we took off, a young woman standing by the rail with me said, "I suppose this has something to do with your family." Her accent was so veddy superior sounding, so provoking I immediately wished her overboard, but I only nodded while the boat chugged over the dark waters of Loch Lomand. We headed toward one of the many heavily wooded little islands sprinkled about the lake. Inveruglas held huge chiseled gray rocks, the remains of stone walls that had tumbled down. Possibly parts of a small castle-fortress destroyed by Cromwell's troops, they were the only true remains of the clan's holdings. In old prints, tall sections of the walls survive.

On the Island Ivaugh I found a foxglove, a narrow pink flower that just fit the tip of a finger. Both islands were as dark as the lake's water, over-grown, difficult to push through, and in the weakening light and rising wind, gloomy. The waitresses, willing to receive any discoveries second-hand, remained on the boat. Wearing the foxglove over one finger tip still, I took it back to Arrochar to press in my passport and show Grandfather McFarland; I doubted he'd be much interested in a flower, but he'd like knowing it came from the Island Ivaugh.

MacTavish drove us to the hotel and met us again that night at Miss Sheena's where we sat around her kitchen table, a light bulb dangling over it, and drank Scotch neat as if it were an after dinner liqueur. Although I was twenty-two and Joe twenty-four, both of us grew up in bourbon-drinking states; we'd never tried Scotch without water. Miss Sheena poured only a little in short glasses; still I drank mine too quickly. Climbing around islands in the chilly afternoon, eating a warm supper at the hotel, topping it off with Scotch, so relaxed me, I let my head droop on Miss Sheena's kitchen table.

"Oh, Lassie, don't be going to sleep on us," said MacTavish.

I lifted my head to ask for water, and as soon my husband finished his drink we walked back to the hotel. I leaned on his arm while staring up at a full moon.

"Do you know they used to call the moon here McFarland's lantern?" he said. "MacTavish told me they were great cattle thieves, and generally they worked by moonlight."

I thought of his Grandfather McFarland waiting out there on the nearly treeless high plains of the Texas Panhandle for news of his ancient history.

"Are you going to tell Granddad?"

"Sure. He'll love it."

<hr/>

Just before we caught the bus for Edinburgh late the next morning, Miss Sheena handed me a great bunch of light purple Scotch heather tied with a plaid ribbon.

She'd succumbed, as many of us do, to the great plaid monster, born inside the borders of Scotland

and living all over the world in the shape of kilts, ties, mufflers, bolts of fabric. You can buy clan tartans by the yard in dress or hunting colors, in factory chemically dyed "modern" or the softer "ancient" or even something called "muted" colors. On our way back to Germany, we stopped in Edinburgh where I bought enough of the McFarland ancient dress tartan to make a dress and cover a chair. Later I learned that tartans, which gained popularity by George IV's royal visit to Edinburgh in 1822—he was the first English king to appear in a kilt—weren't associated with particular clans. Until then people tended to wear plaids woven in their area. I rather liked the idea of being able to choose whatever was personally appealing. On the other hand, the idea of belonging to a clan and wearing its tartan could be just as appealing, depending on whether you're feeling immensely individualistic, simply like certain colors and patterns, or want to show clan loyalty. The Victorians, led by their Queen's interest in all things Scottish, bought little tartan souvenir boxes for snuff, even tiny plaid-covered New Testaments, letter openers, and napkin rings, all ephemera now wafting about to be found in an antique dealer's shop or on ebay.

"From me and MacTavish. Come back to Arrochar," Miss Sheena said as she handed me the heather.

"Oh, we will," we promised, but it was 1989, thirty-three years in the future, when we were following Boswell and Johnson's 1773 *Tour to the Hebrides* before we returned, and of course both Miss Shenna and MacTavish were gone.

Near Arrochar is the Duke of Argyle's castle, Inveraray, where the famous travelers were invited to dine and, according to Boswell, "Dr. Johnson took much notice of the large collection of arms, which are excellently disposed there." In our day, over 200 years later, the same astonishing collection of muskets, axes, and broadswords covered the wall of the Armoury Hall in intricate patterns—round, semi-circular, and crisscrossed. I couldn't gaze at them without thinking of centuries of wars, and I couldn't help but look up Johnson's further comment, "...let us be glad we live in times when arms *may* rust. We can sit to-day at his grace's table, without any risk of being attacked...."

Arrochar, we found, was full of buses full of day-trippers from Glasgow and the roads full of cars. Except for the mountains, we found the small bit of the country we'd known utterly changed. Commercialization—combined with the crying baby at our B&B—and continuing miserable rainy weather drove us away to the nearest hotel in a larger town nearby. Looking back, I think my reaction was, more than anything else, tainted by the loss of Miss Sheena and MacTavish and the glum weather. It was on this trip, however, that I first understood the appellation, "the dour Scots." Continual rain like that could make anyone dour.

I despaired at the changes until I thought once more of meeting the Campbell—which one I can't remember this many years away—who lived near the top of Loch Lomand. He was a stout man wearing a rumpled everyday kilt—made of five yards of tartan rather than the formal one, which is made of eight yards, I'm told—and belt without any of the accessories. The latter range from a plaid folded over one shoulder, a plain or clan-crested belt buckle, a variety of sporrans—the pouch that hangs in front—special ghillie brogues and hose to kilt pins plus a number of hat designs. My favorite is a large, loose-looking beret with a circular topknot called a "See You Jimmy" cap. Tartan shops educate customers about the many parts of kilt outfits, and military kilts have their own specifications. Even though the kilt has been adopted as a national symbol of Scotland, there are apparently different ideas, excepting military regimentation, about what exactly makes the best combination. Scots who buy a kilt must spend many pounds acquiring the full rig, especially if it's a formal one. Dress kilts, like tuxedos, are for rent, and surely some must be inherited. Women, if they wish, use plaid skirts of different lengths, pleated or plain, topped with a white blouse usually, and a solid colored velvet jacket. Of course when it comes to sashes, belts, purses, and jewelry, they have as many or more choices as men.

The Campbell took particular relish in telling us about an old, old hatred between his clan and the McFarlands. We stood before this kindly person entertaining two tourists, entertaining himself, smiling all the time. And in the years to come, I forgot about the ancient clans' quarrel. It was the man I remembered. White-haired, rather short, stomach bulging above his waistband, he stood on the shore of Loch Lomond, water lapping behind him, a Scot relishing a bit of a story to tell. I thought of MacTavish, so willing to show us the places he knew so well, and always of Miss Sheena standing in the middle of a street in one of the world's capitals announcing who she was.

I held their images in mind when we returned to Arrochar in 2010 to show the McFarland country to our fifteen-year-old grandson, Cameron. This time Barbara Millar, a guide who knew Scottish history well, drove us from Edinburgh. The sun fell brightly on the water while we followed the western shore of Loch Lomand and stopped to gaze once more at Inveruglas, now missing its fortress-like stone remains, removed perhaps for other purposes. On the shore in front of a small restaurant-souvenir shop built in the intervening years, we wandered among people buying postcards, basking in the sun, and eating ice-cream cones. Streaks of early afternoon sunlight shone on water and through every tree on the island, one so small it hardly deserved its long name. The grim gray light we'd seen fifty-four years previously was totally burned away.

We'd just driven by the hydroelectric plant, its cement hulk backed against a hill. Up past that hill was Loch Sloy, but we had no need to see it again, no MacTavish to insist we try, and it was Sunday, not a day we could expect to find someone to let us in. The mountains around us were still green, but they didn't look as shaven as they had before, nor were the little rivulets of water sliding down them. A dry summer, Barbara told us, and explained that the government and various groups of conservationists had installed plantations of quick growing evergreens that could be harvested after twenty years. On some hills she pointed out wide strips of stumps, an odd sight to us. When we first visited the Highlands, the mountains, over-grazed by sheep and red deer, were barren except for a short green or gray-brown cover, depending on the season—a sight existing once "the clearances" began after the Battle of Culloden in 1746. That Scottish loss provoked the disastrous breaking up of the clans, resulting in various periods of mass immigrations to Ireland, Canada, America, and Australia, forced by the beginning of sheep farming preferred by English landlords.

Joe had forgotten the exact location of the church and its accompanying graveyard where he'd found McFarland tombstones so many years previously. We stopped at the Arrochar Hotel, now one of several places to stay in town.

To his inquiry about the church and the McFarlands, the young desk clerk crumpled his newspaper before replying, "I just got here a week and a half ago."

"Where did you come from?" Cameron asked. At fifteen he was far more interested in the people than the past, and for all I know, may have thought his grandparents peculiarly attracted to history.

"Australia." The clerk smoothed his newspaper open again.

Barbara took us back to a church near Tarbet she believed we'd passed on our way to Arrochar.

"We have more pews than people in Scotland now. Secularism has grown. A number of the churches have been de-consecrated and are now hotels, or B&Bs, or pubs."

I'd already noticed a church-like looking pub on the Royal Mile from Edinburgh Castle to Holyrood in Edinburgh and considered how centuries of Catholic vs. Protestant wars either had dissolved in beer, or the pub's architecture was a fanciful irony. The fact that Scotland now has an underage alcoholism problem— England has one also—made the growth of pubs appear even more paradoxical; however, we quickly learned that the number of pubs wasn't the whole problem since cheap alcoholic drinks were readily available to any age consumer in many shops. We'd been turned away from two pubs where we'd decided to go for supper because Cameron, though tall for fifteen, was obviously not yet eighteen and it was after eight P.M., a government established hour, though the purpose escaped us since he was accompanied by grandparents and we could easily go to anything called "a restaurant" where alcohol was also served.

We didn't comment on our doubtful thoughts about churches metamorphosing into bars or pubs in the U.S. Perhaps it had already happened; we knew of churches converted to houses even in Texas. The conversion of churches to pubs, especially in Scotland, a country that had for centuries been steeped in John Knox's rigorous brand of Protestantism, remained difficult to comprehend. Nevertheless when we reached the church we had visited in fifty-six and again in eighty-nine, we found a pub inside. Outside people sat at picnic tables enjoying their pints on this clear, sunshiny Sunday.

We skirted the crowd and walked through a gate marked Ballyhennan Burial Ground leading to a graveyard behind the church-pub. There in deep shade we found one Pharlane, an early source of the name, and many McFarlands, McFarlanes, MacFarlands, some of the dim tombstones, dating as far back as the 1700s. We walked about trying to read the worn stones, calling to each other, "Here's another one."

Joe and Cameron took pictures, though not for genealogical records. We'd known that some of those who never immigrated were there. I searched for Miss Sheena's grave, but couldn't find it behind the pub. In her lifetime, she'd left Scotland for the wider world. Unlike our immigrant branch, she'd returned to spend her last years in the village protected by a prayer, entertained by willingness to welcome strangers, and warmed by a good bottle of Scotch.

Our main interest through the years, I saw, hadn't been centered on tracing ancient history, which others had already done. Most of it meanders through old records and a great deal of Celtic mythology: On www. electricscotland.com, I found, "It is recorded by the greatest of Scottish archaeologists, Chalmers, in his *Caledonia*, quoting from the twelfth-century Simeon of Durham, that the ancestor of the family was the Saxon

Arkil, son of Egfrith. This Arkil, a Northumbrian chief... fled to Scotland to escape the devastations of William the Conqueror...." There are, to be fair, other accounts, for the origins of family names tend to vary. This one takes us back to 1066. Five hundred and forty-four years later, though innumerable wars, misfortunes such as being convicted for theft and robbery, and finally loss of the lands around Arrochar sold for debt, our ancestors immigrated first to County Tyrone in Northern Ireland around 1610, then to America in 1719.

Joe believes the search for the trail is part of the fun. I leave that up to him. The generations who left pictures, letters, and stories interest me more since they gave us something to remember them by, little clues to personalities; beyond this is a heap of multiplication tables. Real genealogists are fascinated by the begats, which takes them to census reports, baptismal and marriage records, court records, wills, and maps. I'm not one of them though I understand the lure of the quest, the desire to untangle the knot, akin in a way to solving a DNA puzzle.

Both of us take pleasure in seeing the country and getting to know a few Scots a bit; being able to ask strangers impertinent questions about themselves and their kin is one way to begin a conversation and satisfies basic curiosity. More than this I think perhaps some people simply like feeling they are part of a clan. Even if it's vague knowledge, perhaps it answers an elemental need to belong to something larger than themselves and their immediate families.

When we returned to Edinburgh, outside one of the tartan shops on Prince's Street one morning, I saw a stand full of little paperback books, each one titled with a clan name. Beside me two young men were staring at them.

A skinny, gray-haired old man, so badly in need of a shave that every whisker showed, waggled a finger toward the pamphlets and moved closer.

"Ninety percent of what they say is sheer malarkey. Mind you, maybe ten percent's the truth."

He kept glaring at the three of us.

Did his outrage stem from some misrepresentation of his own clan's history, or was it just a general anger at the Scottish clans' appeal to gullible tourists or both? Then, feeling it best not to ask him, I stepped inside the store to buy a McFarland plaid muffler to take to our granddaughter in America. We'd already bought ties for all the men in the family.

Ranching On Dry Ground

On top of one of the mesas at the ranch at sunset while looking out above a valley toward other distant blue mesas, the view is a grandiose background for a western movie or a chorus singing, "Oh beautiful for spacious skies." The chorus would be "standing on dry ground."

This ranch I eventually inherited is, by Southwestern measures, a small one spreading over parts of Lampasas and Coryell counties in central Texas. Roughly arrow-shaped, it's located in the northern-most hill country. From horseback in the spring the land resembles a large English park until you get down from the saddle and something bites or scratches you.

There is no running water, not a single creek. The nearest river is about three miles distant. In order to water livestock, we use rain-fed "tanks," as ponds are called here, windmills, and springs when we can find them. We need all these sources, as the average annual rainfall, supposedly 31 inches, is just a number we refer to ironically.

When I first came to Texas, I was 12, a city child who knew nothing about ranches. My stepmother had begun putting hers together in 1940 at the end of the

Depression by buying a number of small places near Evant, her hometown, when land, which had been selling for $26 to $28 an acre, fell to $6 to $8 dollars an acre. Actually, in 1942, she paid the smallest amount she would ever have to pay, only $5.76 an acre. Though prices slowly went up, she kept piecing small parcels together until she had enough to lease to her brother to run cattle on. After she married my father, he added 160 more acres Mother called "the G.I. pasture" since he bought it via the Texas Veterans' Land Loan Program in 1957. With this addition, and 33 cares my husband, Joe, added using the same program, we thought the ranch was about 1400 acres.

Then in 1992 the Texas Land Office made the most maddening discovery: we had, in legal terminology, a vacancy. Our ranch surrounded 33.22 acres belonging to the state. Exactly how this happened—careless surveyors, bad copyists, faulty corner marks—couldn't possibly be traced. (One 1879 survey designated a corner using "a rock mound and a Spanish oak marked E.") If land belongs to the state, the state can sell it to anyone. When Texas joined the union, it held title to all the land originally belonging to the Spanish king, then to Mexico. To us, the Texas Land Office was acting like royalty about those acres in the midst of our west pasture, the one everybody used to enter the ranch. It was as though an ancient quarrel between landlord and peasant had surfaced: Mother had to purchase the state's last hold on our land. After putting together so much cheap acreage earlier, she paid $300.00 an acre to buy the vacancy. It was about half of what my husband had to spend, but it wasn't as dear since it was land locked.

Our family never actually lived on the ranch. My parents' house in Gatesville, thirty miles east, was our headquarters. The first Christmas in Texas, four months after moving there from Tennessee, my brother, Billy, 10, and I received matching boots, factory-made with red leather longhorn heads outlined in front, and reminded we had to wear them at the ranch.

We quickly learned the rules for avoiding rattlesnakes, native dwellers in our dry country; watch where you put your boots, and if you see a snake, run as fast as you can to the nearest grown-up. We spent a lot of time studying the ground. Billy threw rocks to kill rattlers. Fortunately I didn't have to confront one until I was grown. The horse I rode, startled by a rattle, shied and without my reining him, found another path. Although the same rules applied to copperhead and coral snakes, I saw copperheads asleep on top of an old piece of metal only once. I never saw a live coral snake, the deadliest of all, though we learned the doggerel warning about its circular markings: "Red and yellow, kill a fellow. Red and black, venom lack." Water moccasins lived in old tanks; we went swimming only in one new tank the first spring it was built, one of the few years we had ample rainfall. After Joe and I started running the ranch, we encouraged snake hunters to clear the rattlesnake dens in the mesas' limestone rim rock. They misted the sleepy hibernating snakes with gasoline until they crawled out to escape the fumes. After collecting the snakes in tow sacks, hunters took them to rattlesnake round-ups, usually held in the spring in nearby counties. Mercifully I never had to attend one, but I've seen enough newspaper pictures to know men test their bravado by surrounding themselves with rattlesnakes, pushing them away with sticks, and doing other foolish things such as the a recent story of someone getting in a sleeping bag with one. The young snake, full of unused venom, bit the intruder's foot, which had to be amputated to save the man's life. Hunters sell their largest snakes to people who concoct antivenom, the only useful thing except men's hatbands resulting from rattlesnakes, as far as I'm concerned, although I do know they help reduce the rodent population. And I'm also aware ecologists believe the loss of rattlesnakes upsets nature's balance. We find their dens are repopulated; if not every year, at least every other, rattlesnakes crawl back from our pastures to hibernate in the mesas' caves.

Scorpions, we learned as children, usually travel in pairs, "like highway patrol men," our mother said. She was a skillful driver but prone to speeding. The name "redbug" replaced our familiar "chigger" although the bite's formidable itch was the same and they were just as unavoidable, or so we thought. Anti-bug sprays weren't readily available in the forties and fifties. Sometime later we learned you could swallow or bathe in a medicinal looking concoction called "flowers of sulfur" that kept redbugs away. When you sweated it made you smell so sulfurous people kept away too.

Depending on spring rains, more vigorous in the forties before our approximately seven-year drought in the fifties—from 1950 till 1957 though creeping toward us as early as 1947—wildflowers filled the pastures. In over-lapping weeks we'd see bluebonnets, orange paint-brush, yellow and red Indian blankets, yellow Mexican hats with conical-shaped green or brown centers, laven-der horsemint, dark purple and lavender bluebells, tight little bouquets of mountain pinks, a field of coreopsis among the profusion of yellow flowers—so many at once that most people forget their common names and say when asked, "Oh, those are yellow flowers." Many other varieties of flowers bloomed, of course, enough to help fill two volumes of Wildflowers of Texas. Faced with this multitude, we half forgot the short, drab winters and the cruel sun we knew would soon dominate. By 2011 our temperatures varied from 100 to 106 degrees. Around here no one goes to the country to cool off.

We can still pick Mexican plums in the early summer and gather native pecans in the fall. The tank we used for swimming the first year it was scooped out of the earth, and another for fishing, stocked with bass in the good years, dried to mud holes, then simply dried out last year. Clumps of gnarled live oak trees, post oaks, Spanish oaks, elms, walnuts, pecans, hackberries, and a dozen other varieties shade parts of pastures and despite sparse rainfall, fill ravines. For picnics in the for-ties, Mother favored a slope overlooking the new tank, where in the early spring or late fall she would build a small fire to heat the food, something too dangerous,

Carolyn trying on chaps belonging to her new Texas cousin,
Thomas Earl Winters, about 1954.

Billy Culbert, rancher, Carolyn's brother, 1936–1973.

The obdurate windmill, Culbert–Osborn ranch.

and forbidden in drought years when whole counties and those adjacent are under burn bans. On Sunday afternoons our father taught Billy how to shoot, a .22, and later, a shotgun. I had no interest in shooting, or in my uncle's steers. I'd walk in the opposite direction to find the bones of a herd of Angora goats that had died right after shearing on top of a mesa when a sudden northern blast killed them all, or to poke around the ruins of the one remaining house site and its defunct windmill in the same pasture, a perfect place for the curious to investigate. My searches yielded only old brown snuff bottles or clear sun-glazed bottles and I would wonder about the people who took the snuff, or used "Horlick's Malted Milk Lunch Tablets," or drank from a bottle impressed with the words, "YOU CAN'T BEAT IT," some kind of whiskey I guessed. Did the crumbling ruin of an elevated stone cistern ever hold enough water for people to shower? Who used up all the ink in the empty ink bottle? Did anyone my age ever live there?

As much as I might want a house of our own at the ranch, we had none. Neither had Thomas H. Williams, "an indigent Texas Revolutionary war veteran" living in 1881 in Matagorda County near the Texas Gulf Coast. He was one of four veterans to acquire some of our land. Williams had to give the names of the captains he'd served under "in the year 1836 after the invasion" and prove he owned property worth $500 or less. On oath he swore he was "physically unable to support myself" and all he had was "1/2 of a 320 acre tract of land, 1 yoke of oxen, and 1 gun." This, written in a beautiful flowing hand, just as everyone who was literate seemed to write then, on aging light brown paper, is all we know of Thomas H. Williams, for he apparently never lived on his land grant from the state; instead it was assigned to agents in Austin who sold the patent to Hyman Blum of Paris, France for an unknown price 45 years after the war with Mexico was over. Blum was evidently one of the many middle-men collecting veterans' land certificates; he sold William's reward for helping Texas win its revolution to local settlers for $1.00 an acre in 1901.

Slightly earlier, in 1876, another veteran, a Confederate army survivor named George W. H. McMorris, came to stay on another part of the ranch: he homesteaded 160 acres near today's ranch's entrance. On a site overlooking a valley beside a live oak tree he built a 14 by 14 foot log cabin with a wild mixture of logs—oak, gum, cedar, whatever was long enough—which contained a loft, and a fireplace, where he and his wife raised three children. How five people lived in such a small space, I don't know, but I've always thought the children must have been told to play outside most of the day when they were small. We've located the spot near the cabin where McMorris dug a well, the only available water source for his family. Since homesteads required cultivation, when the children grew older they probably worked with their father within sight of the cabin in a flat, rock-strewn field made richer by soil eroding off the nearby mesa. Before barbed wire, invented in 1873, arrived in our part of the country in the 1890s, perhaps they helped gather the rocks for a now toppled stone fence, but what was grown there? I'm not sure though I know cotton was the main cash crop then. If McMorris raised cotton, he must have had better rainfall in the 1870s and 1880s than we have now. Partially tumbled down with a half caved-in roof by 1946, what was left of his cabin was used to store hay for winter cattle feeding.

On a slight rise to the south of the log cabin stood the Binfords' house, a little white wooden board-and-batten place probably built later by McMorris, where a family of cedar choppers, a tiny old woman and her three sons, lived. The sons were tall, rangy men with weathered faces, men who seldom spoke, hired by Mother to hand chop cedar on the ranch with double-bladed axes. I didn't fully understand their importance until my husband and I began running the ranch. In our area Ashe junipers, commonly called cedars, grow to tree size quickly and have practically no commercial value. Cattle won't eat them and goats will nibble them away only while the trees are young. Impossible to eradicate—the seeds are continually spread by birds and animals—cedars are a water-depleting scourge as well. A 1997 A&M report shows 33.1 gallons of water per tree per day used by Ashe junipers in our area. That's before our latest drought cycle. Many years after the Binfords' time, my husband, Joe, learned to cut down the small junipers with loppers or a chain saw, a recurrent necessity. He also continually fights mesquite, the thorny, invasive brush that thrives even more in drier south Texas. Though not as numerous as cedar here, mesquite are killed when young by spraying with a diesel-herbicide mixture in the hottest part of the summer, an extremely smelly, disagreeable task.

For the Binfords hard work with low pay was simply the cedar choppers' lot even in earlier years when the wood was used for fence posts. Steel generally replaces cedar now, except for a few corner posts, and Anglo cedar choppers, a tribe of their own, are difficult to find; today Mexican-American crews with chain saws usually take their place.

In the forties and early fifties, I don't know how the four Binfords all managed to live in a three-room plus screened-in back porch house with an outhouse, without electricity or plumbing except one pipe laid from the nearby windmill. The pipe bent at the house's south wall and curled up over a windowsill to a sink. They must have had some sort of stove for heat and for Mrs. Binford to cook on. On our trips to the ranch while we were young, neither I, nor my brother were allowed to go near the house. It was off limits out of respect for the Binfords' privacy according to our mother. I wasn't even tempted to investigate; tall, silent red-faced men with axes were so unspeakably dangerous, they were best left alone.

Finally the Binfords drifted off, perhaps to better accommodations, or perhaps the men joined the army. My father, a World War II veteran who'd served in the Field Artillery, doubted the latter as he thought no matter how dangerous the Binford boys might have looked, they were not bright enough for service.

Billy, by the time he decided to take up ranching about 1963, moved into the Binfords' house while retreating to Gatesville on some weekends, particularly when he needed his washing done. He was a young man at odds with formal education, an ex-paratrooper, ex-vet's assistant, ex-livestock auction worker, ex-rodeo bull-rider. Our parents let him use the ranch lease-free, but there wasn't enough land or water to carry enough cattle and goats to make much of a profit. Gradually he would lease other places.

His years at Mother's ranch, before he died at 36 in a one-pickup wreck in 1973, were full of what seemed to me grubby necessities, but to him, they were, I think now, like the recurrent years of drought, simply part of a rancher's life. When he hired migrant Mexican workers, as many other ranchers did in order to get by, he generally ate whatever they cooked, mostly pinto beans and rice with chilis added for flavor; some days meat from rabbits or armadillos was added. He showered by attaching a piece of hose to a spigot on the windmill, mended barbed wire fences broken by deer that hadn't jumped quite high enough, learned to build new fences on rocky ground—another continual necessity—rode pastures checking on and doctoring cattle, designed and helped build a new corral, shored up the pole barn once again, drove to auctions to buy or sell livestock. Windmills, one of our main defenses against drought, habitually need repair. One on top of a mesa was knocked over and totally dismantled by a tornado that left the tower still standing with its fan's blades, partially overgrown with weeds on the ground, a reason Billy often searched for springs. He discovered the best spring on the ranch at the far north end, underneath a big hackberry and two large cedar elms, where he found a trickle of water and piped it to run steadily to a trough connected to a another trough, connected to a third trough, all of them sitting at odd angles to each other. The trees' trunks and limbs, metal troughs, concrete blocks, pipes and supporting wires all jumbled together, look like a working model of a contemporary art installation. It is an art to somehow manage to weave three awkward six-foot long straight troughs through three trees to make a useful watering place. Just moving those empty troughs to the site was a problem.

The spring is not easily visible from the mesa above. It's hidden within shear rock walls and was found either by prying open a seldom-used wire gate at the northernmost corner of the ranch and hiking up to the site, or by clambering down over rocks and weeds on one side of the wall. To move the troughs in, Billy had to pry open the gate, another difficulty since it hadn't been used for years and was so rusted he probably cut it apart and rebuilt it later.

I'm not sure exactly how he found the spring. I imagine him tying his horse to a tree on top then half-sliding, half-climbing down, as we do now, to reach the mossy wet rocks below. He could have heard tales about the spring from people in Evant, the nearest town, population 550 at its height, withered to 379 in 2010. Supposedly during the Depression, an old man lived in a tent on the mesa and used the spring below as his only water source. In our dry country, springs are to most people such a mysterious gift they incite stories. I can't help but wonder how the old man made it through a hard winter in his tent when the wind blew down from the north so fast the temperature could drop to freezing in an hour.

⊷━✦━⊷

After the loss of my father in 1968 and my brother in 1973, my husband and I decided to venture into a cattle partnership with my mother. For me it was a real venture since I'd never really learned much about ranching. As we grew older, the ranch definitely became my brother's territory and I didn't interfere. I knew, however, it was important to keep Mother occupied: she was spending too much time driving from Gatesville to visit my father's and brother's graves in a little country cemetery near Evant. And I slowly became more curious about how something so remote from my experience might be done. I was already involved in teaching English part time at the University of Texas in Austin, looking after three children, and writing when I could while my husband was practicing law in downtown Austin. We lived ninety miles south of the ranch. To him, an hour and a half's drive wasn't too far; to me the more we discussed the possibility, the more it appealed.

Joe, because he grew up on a stock farm in the Texas Panhandle, was familiar with cattle. I had it all to learn, even the basic language like cow-calf operation, which had no medical connotation: it just meant we would own cows nursing their calves approximately eight months before they were weaned and sold. The next part of the cycle was stockers, those weaned calves that were matured on wheat or grass pastures at other people's ranches. They could be slaughtered after six or eight months, producing grass-fed beef, but the majority generally moved to the feeder stage to be fattened, usually in a feedlot for their last six months. My uncle and brother ran stockers, buying each fall and selling each spring. My mother, Joe, and I chose the cow-calf stage since there was less risk. The volatile beef market could leave a stocker broke if it was low at the time one had to sell. If this happened to us, we might have to take a loss on calves, but we'd still own the cows to produce more offspring another year, an optimistic view of motherhood, I decided. First we had to find the cows, but there were no herds readily available in the country nearby, and once we'd made the decision, we were in a hurry to restock.

Despite Joe's background and familiarity with cattle, together we made one of the worst mistakes we could have; we went to south Texas to buy cows. I thought earlier it might have been a pleasure simply to leave the ranch empty of everything except wildlife, but I knew Mother wouldn't hear of it. Unused acres are too great a luxury to those who've struggled to buy them and the idea of putting land to work was deeply ingrained in her generation. Joe reminded me, owners need the tax break given to agriculture use, and vacant land has its own set of problems including being a continual fire hazard. We knew how frightening a fire on dry land could be.

Late one hot summer afternoon, just as we drove from the ranch to the highway, we saw smoke curling on the horizon. Mother, apparently intuitively aware her place was burning, led the way to the threatening gray signal—set we supposed, by the magnifying effects of sun on broken glass. With the help of the Evant Fire Department, it was quickly contained before it reached gullies covered with cedar. Because of the explosive effect of fire on the oily cedar, a disastrous spread via sparks would have been inevitable. Indians, Comanches probably, purposefully set dry grass on fire in order to attract more buffalo who preferred to eat the new green shoots; Indians obviously had neither fences to burn nor neighbors to consider. And did the cycles of drought we've known exist in Indian days?

We drove down to Uvalde on the border to meet a cattle owner and his agent, two men called Shirley and Carol. We already knew men called June and Francis, so in our experience the custom of giving boys girls' names wasn't novel, we'd just never met two of them together. Our foreman, we'd noticed, customarily named bulls after the men who sold them to us. This time we somehow forgot the sellers' names.

After inspecting cattle from the front seat of Shirley's pickup, we bought two bulls, a hundred mother cows, and their calves for $525.00 a pair, Herefords with Charolais-Hereford calves, some showing a bit of Brahma mix in the pointed tips of their ears. All of them looked good in their part of the country. We didn't object to the mixture since, in theory, hybrid vigor results from crossing. They arrived at our place in three double-decker trucks, were unloaded, and driven to the nearest tank. It had been a good spring and all the tanks were full. I thought the windmill was working; its fan blades were creaking in the wind, but I soon realized no water was being pumped. The fan was simply running free while the water remained underground, my first lesson in the obduracy of windmills. First you have to know what a sucker rod is; then check closely to see if it's moving. It's as if windmills are made to fool anyone watching. Halfway up the tower a scissortail flycatcher, her salmon pink sides barely showing, sat on her nest, her long tail shooting west and her head turned east. Another bird's nest was built beneath the point where the fan joined the tower. It blew to the ground as I watched, and inside I found one mottled green egg. The same day I saw two pair of quail strutting in the yard of the Binfords' old house; soon after, we jumped three jackrabbits and two cottontails; an armadillo, in its half-blind way, ambled across a corner of the pasture. Mother pointed to a horned toad sunning itself near the road, and a neighbor told us a flock of wild turkeys roosted on the east side of one of the mesas. I remembered my father hunted dove and quail on the place every fall. Since the last of Billy's stock was removed, it seemed we'd been running a wildlife refuge.

We'd spent a previous morning riding the perimeter fences of the ranch on horseback and found a fawn, its spots showing in the sunlight while the doe ran off, supposedly tempting us to follow her; a female quail used the same tactic, dragging one wing on the ground to lead us away from her nest, both obeying the instinctive urge to protect their young. I leaned down by my borrowed horse's sweaty neck to watch the almost invisible quail moving noiselessly through the grasses. Later, one early morning ride we saw two bobcats bounding across a pasture. We didn't see coyotes although we could hear them howling at night.

I would have liked to spend days riding around the ranch exploring, but we had to find a windmill man, a fast-fading livelihood since submersible electric pumps are now more widely used. Floyd and Frances Parr, our new foreman and his wife, the two most indispensable people we'd found, directed us to Mr. Perkins who lived near them in Evant. Without contact with people in the area who'd lived there for years, we knew it would be impossible to run a ranch from Austin. Floyd and Frances had been raised on ranches, owned a small ranch themselves, and were willing guides.

Mr. Perkins lived in a house with a porch facing U.S. 281, a highway running from north to south through the state. First we needed to speak through the screen door to Mrs. Perkins who didn't understand what place we were talking about.

We'd always called it "the ranch," a futile description I soon realized, so I stated the whole connection, "I'm Mabel Winters Culbert's daughter, Billy Culbert's sister."

"Oh it's the Billy Culbert place."

Country people have their own place designations. They forgot, or perhaps never knew, it was Mother's ranch. Legal definitions of ownership aren't important; who runs it is. Once this was established, Mrs. Perkins became helpful; she called around to locate Mr. Perkins while we admired her enormous vegetable garden from the front porch. The only seat was a claw-footed bathtub painted yellow, one side cut away revealing a lank cushion about six inches above the floor. In drought-ridden country, it seemed a perfect statement of décor.

Mr. Perkins, himself, looked a bit like an elf; he was a small wiry man dressed in dark green work clothes. He sat on a step, I sat next to him, and Joe hunkered on the ground. No one tried to sit in the bathtub. We soon discovered Mr. Perkins had been my mother's student when she taught at a country school near Evant in the twenties. We often ran into someone who'd known Mother, had built a corral for my brother, worked for my uncle.

To Mr. Perkins we spoke of various windmills on the ranch and springs.

"I'd rather have a good spring than a windmill any day," he said.

Since then I've heard the exact opposite said by other windmill men. Depending on their experience, they thought either a windmill or a spring tended to dry up when most needed. Now I think both do.

Mr. Perkins got our windmill running again. Just as the rest of his dwindling tribe would do in the future, he attempted to explain its inner workings including brass valves, leathers made of cowhide about the size of table-spoons to scoop up the water, and a series of long, long pipes going down to the water's surface a hundred and ten feet below. I understood about half of what he was saying, but I did find, in the years to come, that leathers constantly wear out in our gritty, limestone-suffused water, and require replacement, but only the windmill man seems to know exactly when. Other parts need oiling once a year at least, and the odd-looking metal box covering the gears near the top is called a bonnet because of its resemblance to a woman's old-fashioned sunbonnet, the kind my Texas grandmother had worn.

Mr. Perkins gave me two used brass valves, "to make a candlestick with," he said.

I wondered silently how many candlesticks Mrs. Perkins had.

Shortly after the windmill was repaired and the cattle began to fill out a little, we discovered, unfortunately, some of the cows had developed a taste for prickly pear, a cactus which grows in great numbers in south Texas and, though not quite so numerous on the ranch, is also a large problem in central Texas. Once cows eat pear with the thorns burned off by flame-throwers during droughts, as south Texas ranchers often do, they can become seriously addicted to eating un-prickly pear, so will continue eating them even with thorns on. I'd been told sheep were so dumb they could smother each other to death by huddling too close together in freezing weather, but the "pear-eaters," as Floyd called them, were I was sure, the dumb half of the dumb cow insult.

Reading information published by Texas A&M, we found prickly pear defies destruction except by the use of gallons of chemical spray or a controlled burn, illegal in a drought. The spray required a license, so we got a license and did a bit of spraying before we found we lacked enough hours to do as much as needed. And even if the burn were legal, we don't trust the concept especially since it kills the plant only for a limited time. Now, as it threatens to overtake some pastures, we pay someone to spray prickly pear with the newest A&M recommended poison. As much as we dislike using poison, we'll use it to save a pasture.

The pear-eaters we first bought naturally went on eating it and damaged their stomachs. Soon after that we discovered some of them had a peculiar tick-borne disease called anaplasmosis, which caused them to abort their calves. Trying to understand it, I read a ranchers' magazine listing 21 ways a cow could abort; the 21st item was simply called "more." Even when vaccinated against the disease, cows remained carriers. We eventually sold all of ours to packers, a business that "slaughtered, processed, and packed livestock into meat, meat products and by-products." This is one of those dictionary definitions telling you less than you need to know. In the case of our cows, I suppose packers also sterilized the anaplasmosis-diseased carcasses before turning them into dog food, one of the "by-products."

We learned from Floyd and our vet that anaplasmosis existed in herds nearby, exactly whose we didn't know, so we discovered also that ranchers can be secretive about causes of their cows' deaths.

We began again after requesting help from the nearest U.S. Department of Agriculture office, the bank that loaned us enough money to buy more cows, and my mother who grew up helping her father ranch and was familiar with the multiple risks of raising cows and calves. This time we waited until we could buy stock from reliable local ranchers.

Touring the ranch later with one of the USDA agents, we realized our pastures were over-grazed. In this part of the country a cow and calf together require approximately 23 acres to thrive through dry and wet years. We had a horror of over-grazing. Too often we'd heard of cattlemen over-stocking a place thereby reducing the native grasses. The ranch has numerous species of grass, however our cattle principally graze buffalograss, rescuegrass, and blue grama. Unfortunately we knew we were seeing a lot of inedible broom weed, those dainty yellow flowers coloring pastures in the fall, a sure sign of over-grazed land. Because the main product of ranch land is grass, we had to save it.

We'd already finished a brush-clearing program on the G.I. land; the Binfords' cedar chopping years didn't include it. Our son's three hundred Angora goats and my own multi-colored Spanish goats—at least a hundred of them—were turned loose there to eat the cedar down. Both types of goats were dual purpose; the Spanish goats' kids were sold for meat, mainly to Chinese, Arab, and other immigrant markets, while the Angora goats produced enough mohair—augmented by a generous government support price—to pay for our son's college tuition. Unfortunately we discovered when the goats moved to other pastures in the winter they chose to eat grasses needed for cattle since the green shoots of brush they preferred were dormant. We sold all the goats. And we reduced the cow numbers from a hundred to sixty. The pastures began recovering.

In the meantime, Joe became interested in the original tall grasses grazed almost to extinction. With whatever help available, and most times alone, in Mc-Morris' old field he sowed Indian grass, big and little bluestem, and switch grass. We were rewarded when in the fall bluestem and Indian grass stood more than seven feet tall. Because we cut down our stock numbers, the long suppressed tall grasses, especially the little bluestem, also emerged in other parts of the ranch. My mother, who died in 1994, did not live to see the tall grasses. I'm sure she would have approved just as she approved of the log cabin restoration, the well we had drilled—run by a dependable submersible pump—and the ranch house we built with her in 1974 on the site McMorris once homesteaded.

We needed to be able to rely on a water supply at the house, especially since for years we'd known we couldn't expect reliable rainfall on the pastures, a loss culminating in 2010 when the worst drought since we'd started ranching in 1973 began. The *Austin American Statesman* reported, "The 12 months from October 2010 through September 2011 were the driest for that 12 month period in Texas since 1885, when the state began keeping rain-fall records."

Without spring and summer rains, grasses in our pastures weren't growing sufficient forage, and we were running low on stock water. By 2013 we'd culled the cattle down to 52. Cows need approximately ten gallons of water a day, more or less depending on the heat and the size of the animal; bulls and cows nursing calves need more. In drought years the tanks generally dry out first, then the weak springs quit running. To compound the problem, that year our one working windmill broke, and the people we relied on for repairs proved unreliable. We'd drive up from Austin, stop in Lampasas on the way to the ranch, and confront the placid looking woman who tried to soothe us.

First: "We've had to order a part." (We knew such orders took awhile and decided to wait two weeks.)

Second: "The man who usually does this kind of work is sick." (She explained on our second visit and we considered this plausible.)

Third: "We're overcome with people needing help." (By this time we were overcome with impatience.)

At last, after much discussion, especially since the Lampasas workers had dismantled and hauled the mill to their shop, we hired someone else to truck the broken windmill to another repair place in another county.

In 2011 our son William decided to improve a spring, one Billy had already tried to extend. Where water first seeped, as usual below a mesa's rocks, Billy had set a pipe leading to a large concrete trough, which was generally over-flowing. To capture the over-flow, William's workers designed an addition, a long curving native limestone wall to contain the water. From the south side the wall looked like stonework on a medieval castle. In some seasons it contained enough water to form a pond reaching to the west and spilling over in a small waterfall to the ravine below. In the driest part of the drought, all that water retreated to the old concrete trough.

To find out the volume of water in the other spring Billy had discovered in the GI pasture, I held an empty quart measure under the first pipe while Joe kept his eyes on his watch. The per quart average was 32 seconds, which is 128 seconds per gallon. There are 86,400 seconds in a 24 hour day, so 86,400 divided by 128 equals 675 gallons of water per day from that spring, enough to water 67 cows a year during the worst drought we'd ever experienced.

Our only problem: There wasn't enough grass in that small pasture to support even ten cows. Leaving the gate open wouldn't work either because the spring was too remote from the other pastures. Salt and other minerals are easily delivered as is additional feed, but the necessity of a nearby water supply is primary.

Floyd's spring, one he discovered in a larger pasture, and yet another spring above a pecan grove—each measuring about 474 gallons per day—have carried us through the drought so far. But for the first time since we began ranching, we are worrying about having enough water for the cattle. Drought has ruled so long we must drill another well and raise another windmill. Obviously we have spring water; however, exactly how plentiful water collected in various springs is we don't know. All of our springs are on or near tops of mesas; according to our son's knowledge of geology, we have typical "perched aquifers" which are trapped between a thin layer of limestone and dolomite, but these have little stored reserves unless replenished by rain. Nor do we know exactly how many others depend on the Trinity aquifer, the underground water formation in our area.

We do know more houses are being built; consequently more wells are drilled and reports from the Texas Water Development Board state the fact that pumping from the aquifer "far exceeds recharge." So on this small ranch in Central Texas, our need for stock water from tanks, windmills, and springs continues, and our concern about climate change grows. Inflation and recreational value have driven up the price since my mother's first purchase. What my father used to call "goat acres" in a faintly derisive tone, and where he used to hunt dove and quail, is now also valuable for deer hunting. We see few of these birds now, and like most other ranchers, are worrying about what is happening to them. Drought, disease, and the invasion of fire ants—since quail nest on the ground—are the prevalent answers. On the other hand, after being hunted to extinction by original settlers by the 1890s, whitetail deer began to drift back to our country from the south. In 1967 my father happened on a deer bed, wild gasses and small plants pressed in an oval shape under one of the native pecan trees. Forty-five years later a seasonal lease can bring as much as $1500.00 per hunter. We never lease. Even in the midst of a record drought, we still have too many deer, hunted only by our family and friends and Frances and Floyd's two sons. Perhaps this is a landowner's unique form of selfishness, but it's also a way of preventing wild shots from strangers' guns hitting our cows and calves.

Like everyone else who owns land, we know we are only caretakers, but our ancient right to choose who will set foot on the ground remains. The old furious forms of admonition still hold: "Get out of our house! Get out of our yard! Get off our land!" We may forgive those who trespass against us, yet we state, "No trespassing." Though the ranch is often dry, difficult to profit from, and expensive to maintain properly, it remains ours to look after until we pass the privilege to the next generation. And, unless there is a formidable climate change including far more rainfall, they will also inherit all the land's limitations.

About the Author

Carolyn Osborn gradu-ated from the University of Texas at Austin with a B.J. degree in 1955, and an M.A. in 1959. She has won awards from P.E.N., the Texas Institute of Letters, and a Distinguished Prose Award from *The Antioch Review* (2003). Her stories have been included in *The O. Henry Awards* (Doubleday, 1990) and *Lone Star Literature* (Norton, 2003), among numerous other anthologies. She is the author of two novels, *Contrary People* (Wings Press, 2012) and *Uncertain Ground* (Wings Press, 2009), and four collections of short stories, including *A Horse of Another Color* (University of Illinois Press, 1977), *The Fields of Memory* (Shearer Publishing, 1984), *Warriors & Maidens* (Texas Christian University Press, 1991) and *Where We Are Now* (Wings Press, 2014). The Book Club of Texas published an illustrated, specially bound edition of her story, *The Grands* (1990). In 2009, she received the Lon Tinkle Lifetime Achievement Award from the Texas Institute of Letters.

Wings **Press** was founded in 1975 by Joanie Whitebird and Joseph F. Lomax, both deceased, as "an informal association of artists and cultural mythologists dedicated to the preservation of the literature of the nation of Texas." Publisher, editor and designer since 1995, Bryce Milligan is honored to carry on and expand that mission to include the finest in American writing—meaning all of the Americas, without commercial considerations clouding the decision to publish or not to publish.

Wings Press intends to produce multicultural books, chapbooks, ebooks, recordings and broadsides that enlighten the human spirit and enliven the mind. Everyone ever associated with Wings has been or is a writer, and we know well that writing is a transformational art form capable of changing the world, primarily by allowing us to glimpse something of each other's souls. We believe that good writing is innovative, insightful, and interesting. But most of all it is honest.

Likewise, Wings Press is committed to treating the planet itself as a partner. Thus the press uses as much recycled material as possible, from the paper on which the books are printed to the boxes in which they are shipped.

As Robert Dana wrote in *Against the Grain,* "Small press publishing is personal publishing. In essence, it's a matter of personal vision, personal taste and courage, and personal friendships." Welcome to our world.

Colophon

This first edition of *Durations*, by Carolyn Osborn, has been printed on 55 pound Edwards Brothers Natural Paper containing a percentage of recycled fiber. Titles have been set in Isadora type, the text in 13 point Adobe Caslon type. All Wings Press books are designed and produced by Bryce Milligan.

On-line catalogue and ordering:
www.wingspress.com

Wings Press titles are distributed
to the trade by the
Independent Publishers Group
www.ipgbook.com
and in Europe by
www.gazellebookservices.co.uk

Also available as an ebook.